Should divorced people be treated like . . .

SECOND CLASS CHRISTIANS?

A New Approach to the Dilemma of Divorced People in the Church

MICHAEL A. BRAUN

INTERVARSITY PRESS
DOWNERS GROVE, ILLINOIS 60515

InterVarsity Press is the book-publishing division of InterVarsity Christian Fellowship, a student movement active on campus at hundreds of universities, colleges and schools of nursing. For information about local and regional activities, write Public Relations Dept., InterVarsity Christian Fellowship, 6400 Schroeder Rd., P.O. Box 7895, Madison, WI 53707-7895.

Distributed in Canada through InterVarsity Press, 860 Denison St., Unit 3, Markham, Ontario L3R 4H1, Canada.

The Scripture quotations contained herein are from the Revised Standard Version of the Bible copyrighted 1946, 1952, 1971 by the Division of Christian Education of the National Council of the Churches of Christ in the U.S.A. and are used by permission. All rights reserved.

Cover background: Roberta Polfus

ISBN 0-8308-1280-6

Printed in the United States of America ♾

Library of Congress Cataloging-in-Publication Data

Braun, Michael, Th.M.
     Second-class Christians?: a new approach to the dilemma of
divorced people in the church/Michael A. Braun.
          p.   cm.
     Includes bibliographical references and indexes.
     ISBN 0-8308-1280-6
     1. Divorce—Religious aspects—Christianity.   2. Church work with
divorced people.   I. Title.
     BT707.B73   1989
     241'.63—dc20   89-31815
                                                                      CIP

17	16	15	14	13	12	11	10	9	8	7	6	5	4	3	2	1
99	98	97	96	95	94	93	92	91	90	89						

*To the brothers and
sisters of Community
Church, 1970–1985,
who taught me the
Scriptures.*

Acknowledgments

I am deeply indebted to Dr. Robert Culver, who read the entire manuscript and made invaluable observations. Dr. Loren Wilkinson and his wife, Mary Ruth, read the manuscript in the midst of a busy sabbatical and gave me a great deal of encouragement. The elder board of Community Evangelical Free Church gave many hours to discussing with me the issues in this volume. I hope this book is the richer for their kind efforts. Richard Parker, who often agreed with my thinking, and Dr. Dana Focks, who often did not, were a great help to me. My mother, Barbara Braun, quietly and graciously corrected the entire work. Finally, my wife Susan, my biggest fan, sharpest critic and best friend, made this entire project both a joy and a challenge for me.

In addition to those mentioned above I would like to thank so many others, too numerous to mention, who shared in my life as I worked through the ideas of this book. Much of the credit for what is good in this volume goes to them. Needless to say, all the goofs, gaffes and glitches (that which my son's fellow Cadets refer to as synapse lapses) are solely my responsibility.

—1—
Our Long National Nightmare

At the end of what once seemed to be an endless struggle, Leon Jaworski, the Watergate special prosecutor, finally packed his briefcase and flew back to Texas and to the church that had so long and so faithfully supported him in prayer. An "unindicted co-conspirator" left the White House in a final, painful helicopter flight as president, and a new president from Michigan faced a weary American public. The nation seemed to heave a collective sigh of relief when he spoke these now famous words: "Our long national nightmare has ended."

But the fact is that a greater nightmare is stalking the soul of our country. And it is a reality, not a dream. It is a chilling, undeniable fact. It is a cancer eating its way into the very center of our country's personal strength and human resources.

It is called *divorce.*

Divorce was once a recognized evil in our country. But today it seems to be a way of life.[1] It affects us in ways we can't begin to imagine and leaves a deep and lasting impression on the nature of our homes, the development of our children and even the fellowship of our churches.[2]

Every day across America literally thousands are lured into the easy solution of a "no fault" divorce. They fall victims to the false promises and contemporary myths of modern life. In countless situations their quick decisions and short-lived freedom swiftly turn to long-term guilt.

Sadly, for many divorced people caught in this turmoil of mind and soul, biblical churches are the last places they would go for help.

They may be lonely, spiritually hungry and burdened with shame and guilt. Nevertheless, divorced people often avoid the company of Christians. They feel, with some justification, that they could not endure the rejection, the condemnation and the hopelessness expressed in certain Christian teachings regarding divorce.

If we can open avenues of approach, if we can communicate concern and compassion to this increasingly large and needy segment of our population, then a floodgate of healing and hope will be released in our country. As the church of Jesus Christ, armed with the saving message that Jesus himself brought into the world, we are intended by God

to be a vast reservoir of hope, help and healing—offering places of comfort and rest in a careless world.

A View from the Communion Table

One of the things I enjoy most as a pastor is being seated with the congregation around the communion table on a Sunday morning. We usually sit in large semicircles with the table in the center. I enjoy looking out on the sea of faces as we share our thoughts and prepare ourselves for the Lord's Supper.

The Lord Jesus, on the night he was betrayed, took bread...

We generally allow the parents to decide at what age their child can take communion and on those communion Sundays we cancel the programs for the older kids. The result can be a little chaotic, but it helps our communion time to center around the family in a special way.

As I look out on all those faces—people sitting together as one church family—time after time, God speaks to me and quickens my love for them. They belong to God, and that makes them remarkably important. It cost God a great deal to reclaim them. I can see them now, in my mind's eye, waiting, intense, caught up in the moment. When someone asks me how I like the pastorate, I feel like saying, "I love the view."

He broke it and said, "This is my body which is given for you..."

There's Mary. She and her husband have adopted four small children afflicted with spina bifida, a congenital and crippling birth defect of the spine. The biological parents wanted to throw them away at birth. Mary and her husband have given them a family. The kids, in wheelchairs, sit with their Mom and Dad and wait for the communion bread to be given them.

Mary and her husband are willing to endure the stress which handicapped children often place on a marriage. They shoulder the hardships and sacrifices as an offering to God. Their marriage, though often challenged by unimaginable difficulties, is a strong one.

Nearby Tim and his wife sit with their four natural children and their new foster son. The child was born deaf. Tim and his wife feel the relationship they have is close and the home God has given them is a loving one. They want to minister through their home life. There are many abandoned children that our society keeps producing and discarding. But one of them now sits with God's people, and is learning, slowly, that Jesus loves him.

Next to them are Joe and Carol, a young couple without children who give a good deal of their time and money counseling young women who, under the stress of an unwanted pregnancy, might try to kill the only baby they will ever have.

They hold the bread in their hands.

Nearby, Ken and Sandra bow their heads in prayer as Jesus' familiar words are repeated once again.

Take, eat . . .

A few months back Sandra was ready to end their marriage. She was going to take their little girl to another state. Ken cried out to God. Sandra trusted Christ. The Lord is healing their hearts.

The bread is in their mouths. They chew it slowly, thoughtfully.

Across the aisle are Ted and Joan, married nearly fifty years. They watch intently as I pour the wine out into the glass.

This cup is the new covenant in my blood . . .

Behind them is Bonnie. Next to her is her son Bill. Fifteen years ago Bonnie's husband walked out on her. Their little boy was three years old. Her husband never came back. Drugs. Threats. Betrayal. Adultery. The husband visited our church once with his girlfriend. Little Bill couldn't understand why Daddy's new girlfriend had a son who called his own father "Daddy."

"Little" Bill is over six feet tall now. He is a merit scholar studying at the university. His mom is sitting with her new husband, a godly man who loves the Lord and his new wife very much.

This do in remembrance of me . . .

I once told the church not to be intimidated by people who claim to be "super spiritual." I tried to emphasize our equality in Christ by reminding them that there are no real heroes. The only heroes are in the funny papers.

I was wrong. I know that now.

There are a lot of heroes out there, unheralded and unsung. They fight courageous battles every day. They face terrible odds, often alone. They bear heavy burdens and realize remarkable accomplishments, like raising children in a safe and loving atmosphere. They are threatened and sometimes frightened, get discouraged and disappointed. They suffer, but yet they endure.

The cost of their heroics is the steady erosion of the best years of their lives. But they pay it gladly. Contrary to the talk-show values of our "me generation," they expend the vigor of their youth and young adulthood on others instead of on themselves. Sometimes they sacrifice job opportunities and material possessions and pleasures. They honor their mothers and fathers and stay faithful to their husbands and wives. They are combatants in the noble but silent struggles of life. They are learning to be faithful, just like their God.

You proclaim the Lord's death until he comes . . .

In a generation of faithless fathers and careless mothers, in an age of shattered marriages and desertions of the heart, these people are heroes. They are heroes of whom "the world is not worthy." A cup of challenge and hardship may be their portion for now, but a victorious hero's chalice awaits them.

Drink ye all of it . . .

Christians today in our country need to be heroes. The enemy is very strong. A battle is raging and many people are afraid.

Onward, Christian Soldiers

As always the enemy is the world, the flesh and the devil. But the real battleground today is the family, that divinely established guardian of our minds and bodies and the very backbone of the church of Jesus Christ. Not only does the family provide the church with the raw stuff of humanity from which the church is built, but the family also is the very source of all the church's most precious conceptual models through which we envision God and humans together. Both our Father in heaven and his uniquely begotten Son watch over our brothers and sisters until the time when we are presented in eternity as the bride of Christ. We, the church, the "household of God" and the "pillar and bulwark of the truth," understand the deepest truths of heaven through the model of the family on earth.

The church, then, is unavoidably drawn into Satan's war against the family. Though at times it may try to act as a neutral observer in the conflict, the church is, in fact, a combatant.

The spiritual warfare goes on and the cries of anguish from the wounded echo in the hearts of those who care. It's a war, and the prize of battle is very great indeed. The two battle zones—the church and the family—desperately need each other's comfort. The family and the church are inextricably bound together in the conflict.

One of the greatest wounds inflicted in this clean and quiet war against family and church is divorce. And while those in real agony cry out, the strategy of God's people seems confused and in disarray.

A few years back at a conference of Christian pastors I met an old school friend. We walked out of the meeting room together. He was furious. The subject of the meeting was the question of whether or not a divorced man could ever serve as a pastor of a church. The tone of the meeting was strident, and the majority seemed about to move to the simplest and strictest rule: If any man has ever been divorced, whether before or after his conversion, he would not be allowed ordination. This was a straight line, a clear statement, but we both felt it was dangerously wrong.

My friend was livid. We talked. For some reason, that day the Lord allowed us to have a very personal conversation. My friend's anger was really reflecting a great sorrow and fear deep within himself.

It seems the year before this young pastor, a husband and father, came very close to having an affair with a member of his congregation. By the grace of God he resisted the powerful temptation. But he was still confused and desperately in need of someone to talk to. He had nearly destroyed his marriage and his ministry. But to whom could he talk? The possibility that a pastor might have marital problems is so threatening to some congregations that it seems to be an unspoken evangelical law that pastors who have marital problems must never admit to them.

There are pastors who live in great fear that their congregations might discover their feet of clay. It is a paralyzing fear, but sadly not an altogether unjustified one. Honest efforts of pastors to seek help so openly could cost them their jobs. In short, the cure could prove worse than the disease.

I'll never forget what this particular pastor said to me that day. Though he was a decidedly unemotional man, tears welled up in his eyes as he looked hard at me: "Mike," he said, "we evangelical Christians are the only army in the world who shoot their wounded."

There certainly is a battle going on around us, but just whom are we shooting at? All too often the church levels its biggest guns at the fallen bodies of its own wounded. It has been said, half in jest, that the Christian who has a problem automatically has two problems. First, there is the problem itself. But next to that is the second problem, which is the unspoken yet overpowering conviction that Christians should never have any problems. We condemn ourselves in this (and are very quick to condemn others) not merely for a particular problem, but for the fact of having a problem at all.

The church, which should be a place of hope and help, a place where problems can be faced openly and solved, so easily becomes a fearful place where we dare not admit to difficulties for fear of critical, even hostile opinions of others.

This has to change.

Jane: The Girl Who Wanted to Be Free

Jane isn't her name, but it'll do. She was a very nice girl, always had been. In fact, she was nearly impeccable. She seemed to do almost everything right, all the time.

Take, for example, the parents she chose for herself. Aristocratic, well-to-do; propriety was their middle name. It was their last name too. Jane and her sisters grew up in very comfortable surroundings. Jane always tried to *do* the right thing and she always seemed to *have* the right things.

As a little girl, Jane was always pleasant. Even as an adolescent she was pleasant. (Well, tolerably so.) Jane knew it paid to be pleasant. If you are nice to people, you can generally get your own way. Jane generally got her own way. As I said, she was very pleasant.

Jane went pleasantly through high school, and equally as pleasantly through college. Her greatest fear was that someone might discover that she wasn't really as pleasant as she seemed. That possibility worried her at times.

After college, Jane took a position with a major corporation. She traveled extensively. In due time, she met a man and fell pleasantly in love. They married and, as time progressed, Jane became the mother of first one and then another little girl. Jane was settling down for a nice, pleasant stay in life.

By this time her husband had established himself well in his university position, the girls were growing up and showing themselves to be quite independent and capable, and so Jane, encouraged by her husband, went back to school. She took a graduate degree, became a professional woman and stepped into a respected position. Jane began a new career of helping others—and watched her own life begin to fall apart.

As one might expect, Jane's life didn't fall apart catastrophically. No, it just sort of unraveled slowly, even pleasantly.

One day Jane announced to her husband that her marriage was no longer fulfilling. She wanted to explore "alternative relationships" and "shape a new lifestyle." Divorce, she informed her husband, was a necessary first step in achieving the greater self-awareness that she longed for.

Self-assertive? Perhaps. But pleasantly so.

It all went very well. In fact, her friends were lavish in their praise for the civilized way Jane and her husband went through a "friendly" divorce. Jane's children, though slightly dizzied over the events, believed their mom and dad fully when they told them that this was a perfectly acceptable thing to do. From time to time the girls felt depressed but they couldn't say just why. They accepted the divorce calmly and joined the long parade of commuter children who shuttle back and forth between the two emerging houses born of one broken home.

Jane's husband did not protest. He felt hurt, but because he was well schooled in the modern values of fractured family life, he understood. He was generous in his support and noncombative in his cooperation with Jane's quest for a new freedom. However, as he put it, he was somewhat of a traditionalist and needed the support of a more singular, if absorbing, relationship. It may be that he was overly insecure. But, being tolerant of others, he accepted that fact in himself. He soon remarried and started a new family.

For some reason, Jane couldn't for the life of her explain why this disturbed her. But it did, a little.

Fresh from a "successful" divorce, Jane began a series of "alternative" relationships. Surprisingly, the old sense of unfulfillment remained, but this time it was accompanied by a new feeling—an increasingly morbid and dominant sense of guilt.

19

Jane went to war against her superego—to no avail. As the guilt deepened, she blamed in turn her middle-class upbringing (upper middle class, to be sure), her middle-class parents, her middle-class values and her middle-class friends.

This accomplished little except to aggravate a growing pain in her own middle. The whole thing was becoming a bit unpleasant.

At the time Jane's guilt began reaching near-panic levels, she was having her latest "alternative" relationship with a professed Christian. He had apparently overcome his strong fundamentalist "hang-ups" about sexual ethics while maintaining an allegiance to its more arcane doctrines.

As a Ph.D. who had served for a time on the faculty of a respected Christian university, Jane's "latest" succeeded admirably in rationalizing his own sexual immorality by a shotgun defense drawing eclectically from the Old Testament. He appealed, randomly, first to levirate practices of "raising up seed," then to patriarchal polygamy, and in turn to David, Solomon, Gomer and Tamar. He avoided Onan in particular and Paul altogether.

He knew his Bible. From time to time he would discourse philosophically, and say with a true Anabaptist suspicion of the state, "What is marriage anyway? A piece of paper!"

He also went to church.

Jane was very confused. She was a lifelong Catholic who had stopped going to church. Maybe church was the answer. She asked her more religious boyfriend if they might attend his church. He wisely demurred, knowing that his small, fundamentalist fellowship would probably take a dim view of this relationship with Jane, in spite of Abraham's indiscretions.

But Jane's guilt and depression deepened. More and more she asked herself, "What have I done? What have I done?" Her children's calm acceptance of their ruined marriage, her ex's civility, her friends' approval—they all burned like the harshest rebukes. God's Word calls it godly sorrow, or conviction. Jane wanted to find God, if he could be found. She decided this meant going to church. With or without her boyfriend, she was going.

Faced with this reality, the boyfriend steered Jane away from his home church into the more comfortable anonymity of an unfamiliar church. So by God's sovereign appointment, one Sunday morning they showed up in our congregation.

The first sermon they heard was on God's view of the sanctity of marriage. Jane heard the gospel for the first time. Over the next few months Jane moved from guilt to repentance and gave herself to Jesus Christ.

As the gospel opened Jane's eyes, it also opened her heart. From the perspective that only God's forgiveness can give, Jane understood her guilt and her sin.

About a year after her conversion, Jane shared her experiences with the church around the communion table one Sunday. This pleasant young woman, with her daughters (now believers) looking on, reminded us all that the world with all its glitter and promises deceives and destroys. Satan, with vicious lies, wants to destroy not only the joy of living but even life itself.

The modern myth about divorce had nearly destroyed her and her children. But she has found sanity and hope in the

Lord Jesus. Jane was indeed broken. And her story of redemption is almost ideal. By God's grace her life was knit back together in a healing and loving community of believers who accepted her and cared for her and taught her God's Word.

Unfortunately, her story is somewhat unusual. So many in our society today buy the Big Lie that says the laws of God governing human life and family are only the relative standards of humans. Our world says you can break these laws with virtual impunity. But God's Word says that if we break his laws, we are the ones who become broken.

Joe: The Man Who Couldn't Go Home Again

I could tell you the sad story of a man I'll call Joe. Joe followed Christ all through high school and college. We were the closest of friends. I was best man at his wedding and he was best man at mine. We were married within a few short weeks of each other, and for the first year of our marriages, the four of us spent a good deal of time together. But then my wife and I packed up our VW, left the familiar surroundings of southern California, and headed off for the Midwest to face the sleet, the snow and the rigors of seminary.

The night my first child was born I called Joe from Illinois to tell him of the happy event. He was glad for us, he said. Then he, from his empty California apartment, told me that his wife had run off with another man.

The events of our lives surround us and serve to reinforce the choices we make, whether good or bad. And sometimes the events of our lives fall in upon us unexpectedly, forever shutting doors we thought would always be open. Now, in the debris of those unexpected twists of life, we find it almost impossible to reopen those doors.

It happened to Joe. After his divorce, Joe withdrew from his Christian friends, more out of embarrassment than defiance. And things began to happen.

Joe's first wife was tragically murdered by the man she had run off with. Joe took the news stoically. But those of us who knew him well saw the guilt and confusion in his eyes. Joe married a second time, to an unbeliever. This marriage ended even more quickly than the first. But there was a little girl now, a daughter Joe loved deeply. He gets to see her once a year for a short time because his second wife moved several thousand miles away after their divorce.

In his sorrow and confusion, Joe had made some choices after his first divorce. He had, rightly or wrongly, closed some doors. Christian fellowship was one of them. Then when things grew so much worse, Joe found the door seemingly nailed shut in the coldness and estrangement of his own heart.

What troubled me in all of this was the ease with which Joe could slip away from the fellowship of God's people. I am not convinced that he is to blame for all of the alienation.

Initially, after his first divorce, Joe was too ashamed to seek out Christian fellowship which had at one time been so important to him. He became more fixed in his choice to avoid the church even after the calamities that followed. To this day, as a school administrator in his mid-forties, Joe lives in a shadow world between his hobbies and his work. At times he wistfully thinks back on the God he once professed to know and the Christian community that once meant so much to him.

Joe lost touch with the church. And I can't shake the feeling that the church was just as happy to lose touch with him. They seemed to be a mutual embarrassment to each other. As Joe's life became more complicated by his sin, the church seemed even less of an option to him. One could say that Joe only has himself to blame, and that may be true, but I'm not entirely convinced. Although Joe's story rests here, perhaps the church's response does not.

Though divorced people as a group form an increasingly large segment of our society, many evangelical churches are out of touch with their special needs. Meanwhile the divorced person may languish in self-imposed exile, avoiding the risks of further condemnation and judgment.

And even among churches who would like to dispel the judgmental image that hovers over them, there is a certain awkward embarrassment about the divorced. One look at a 35-year-old, single parent sitting alone at a church supper should convince us of this.

The lack of special church programs and specialized ministries with the divorced person in mind is often loudly lamented in Christian periodicals. It has become fashionable to do this. But even when a church develops this or that special program for divorced people, alienation can still exist. Special ministries, instead of being avenues back to the heart of church fellowship, can become dead-end streets. The evangelical church often silently continues to keep divorced people, even the divorced people in their own congregations, at arm's length and away from the heart of church fellowship and ministry.

The evangelical church is often guilty of abusing divorced people because it is sadly prejudiced in its understanding of scriptural teaching on divorce. The church may be guilty of failing to minister to divorced people because it is uninformed of the role it is supposed to play in the resolution of conflict in the lives of its people. Finally, the church may be failing in its ministry to divorced people because it has chosen a faulty view of ethical judgment in an era of growing ethical confusion and complexity.

God's people must turn to the Word of God with the courage to use it aggressively and boldly. The line of least resistance is no guideline when people's lives are at stake. Caution and compromise are not the best approaches in a battlefield. Satan's war against family and church is raging around us. To use Luther's phrase, we must be "bold to sin." It is true that involvement in people's problems can become a messy business. Nevertheless the cynical observation of Dylan Thomas should serve as a challenge to the church of Christ: "People with no arms have the cleanest hands." We must run risks in order to rescue people. To this end I have written this book. I pray that it might play some small role in encouraging the church to be the church . . . to encouraging it to get its hands a little dirty.

—2—
Marriage Was Built to Last

*J*esus said that divorce was contrary to the will of God. He taught that God had revealed this to all mankind.

And Pharisees came up to him and tested him by asking, "Is it lawful to divorce one's wife for any cause?" He answered, "Have you not read that he who made them from the beginning made them male and female, and said, 'For this reason a man shall leave his father and mother and be joined to his wife, and the two shall become one flesh'? [Gen 2:24] So they are no longer two but one flesh. *What therefore God has joined together, let not man put asun-*

der." They said to him, "Why then did Moses command one to give a certificate of divorce, and to put her away?" He said to them, "For your hardness of heart Moses allowed you to divorce your wives, but from the beginning it was not so. And I say to you: *whoever divorces his wife, except for unchastity, and marries another, commits adultery.*" (Mt 19:3-9—emphasis mine; see also Mk 10:2-12)

To insure that his moral teaching regarding marriage is understood to be binding on all people, Jesus appeals not to the Hebrew prophets, where convictions against divorce were repeatedly expressed (see Mal 2:16), but to the beginnings of humankind. In referring as he does to Genesis 2:23-24, Jesus is saying in effect that lifelong, monogamous fidelity between a husband and a wife is God's intention for the human race in every society, and in every age. Jesus' position, in stark contrast to the laxity of the prevailing Rabbinic opinion of his day,[1] was all the more remarkable and evidently no small matter of contention between him and popular Jewish ethical teaching. Nevertheless, our Lord is clear—marriage was intended to last a lifetime.

The Danger in Divorce: Actual and Potential

Given Jesus' hard-line stance, the question of divorce is troubling for the Christian from the very outset. Jesus seems to say in Matthew 19 that divorce involves both *actual* and *potential* sin.

The *actual* sin of divorce according to Jesus is the severing, or the attempt to sever, that which "God has joined together" (Mt 19:6). The command is clear—"Let not man put [a marriage relationship] asunder." It is wrong for us to attempt, illegitimately, to undo what God has done. We lack God's authority.

Moreover, we allow the possibility of further sin if we labor under the delusion that we have undone the work of God who has forged the marriage union. God has joined them together. There is then a *potential* sin that awaits those who labor under the false impression that we can arbitrarily break this union.[2]

The *potential* sin of divorce is the possibility of adultery. If one marries again without legitimate grounds to do so, the second marriage, with the assumption that sexual intimacy will accompany it, is in fact an act of adultery. This is the apparent implication of Jesus' direct statements in the Sermon on the Mount: "Every one who divorces his wife, except on the ground of unchastity, makes her an adulteress; and whoever marries a divorced woman commits adultery" (Mt 5:32).

In this passage Jesus tacitly recognizes the unique vulnerability of women in his society. He assumes the necessity of remarriage for the divorced wife because he understands that remarriage may be her only hope for physical survival. In fact her remarriage might be taken out of her hands entirely by her family. Thus Jesus concludes that a husband who divorces his wife *makes* her an adulteress, that is, he shares responsibility for this almost certain calamity.

In the Palestinian environment divorce was generally a male prerogative.[3] So Jesus, without commenting whether it is right or wrong, reflects his awareness of both the woman's unique vulnerability and the man's uncontested prerogatives when teaching on divorce in a Palestinian context.

Paul, on the other hand, will presume on the greater flexibility of the Hellenistic culture when he writes regarding
divorce to the Corinthian church. Paul and Jesus are certainly
not in conflict. In 1 Corinthians 7 the apostle continually
acknowledges the primacy of Jesus in all matters. (Paul calls
Jesus *Lord* no less than seven times in that chapter.) But it
is obvious that the cultural realities of Palestine are reflected
in the Sermon on the Mount, while the more "liberal" cultural realities of Corinth are reflected in Paul's letter.

Consequently Paul advises the departing wife to "remain
single" and, hopefully, "be reconciled." The prospect of the
woman initiating the breakup of a marriage is evidently
more of a possibility in Corinth than in Galilee. And the concern that a divorced woman may well be forced to commit
adultery because of her divorce is apparently less of an in-
evitability in Paul's situation than in Jesus'. It would seem
then that a woman's ability to "remain single" is more of an
option in Corinth than it would be in Galilee. Thus Paul
would write:

> The wife should not separate from her husband (but if she
> does, let her remain single or else be reconciled to her
> husband)—and that the husband should not divorce his
> wife. (1 Cor 7:10-11)[4]

The apostle is not contradicting Jesus here. On the contrary,
he is attempting to apply accurately Jesus' basic teaching
regarding marriage to one of the many possible complexities
that occur in life.

Paul is not suggesting that either marriage partner can
walk away from the marriage with impunity. In fact Paul
says quite clearly that that should not happen. What he ap-

pears to be saying is that when the actual sin of breaking apart a union established by God has already been committed, at least the potential sin of adultery can be avoided if no future marriage is consummated. Therefore Paul says to stay single or else be reconciled.

In either case the reconciliation of the separated husband and wife is desired. However both Jesus and Paul recognized that, tragically, there are times when reconciliation is not possible. The Bible allows for the possibility of divorce in certain circumstances. Though marriage is God's plan for life, the teachings of Jesus Christ offer hope for those caught in the shame and reproach that a broken marriage often brings. God's Word regulates when a marriage bond may or may not be broken in human society.

Death Breaks the Marriage Bond

The conviction capable of broadest acceptance among Christians regarding the severed marriage bond is that Scripture expressly states that death terminates marriage and that a remarriage of the surviving partner is permissible.[5]

A married woman is bound by law to her husband as long as he lives; but if her husband dies she is discharged from the law concerning the husband. (Rom 7:2)

Similar language is employed by Paul in 1 Corinthians:

Are you bound to a wife? Do not seek to be free. . . . A wife is bound to her husband as long as he lives. If the husband dies, she is free to be married to whom she wishes, only in the Lord. (7:27, 39)

Death loosens the bond of marriage and releases the surviving partner to consider the possibility of remarriage.

Though I will say more later, it should be noted here that it is not uncommon for some people to suggest that Romans 7 contains the only valid exemption from the marriage bond. Only death, they say, releases someone legitimately from a marriage bond. This is simply not true, as an examination of Matthew 5 and 1 Corinthians 7 will indicate. It should be noted further that while Matthew 5, Matthew 19, Mark 10 and 1 Corinthians 7 are all direct teaching passages concerning divorce, Romans 7 is not.

Romans 7 concerns itself with the effectiveness of the death of Christ in releasing humans from the demands of the law. Paul mentions divorce in that context only to illustrate another point. That does not mean that what he says is invalid, but what it does mean is that it would be foolish to consider a biblical illustration, applying to an entirely different issue, to be the definitive statement on the issue of remarriage. There are other passages to consider even though their arguments may be more difficult to understand. Romans 7:2 is not God's final word on the question of releasing a person from the marriage bond. But before we look at these other passages, let's look at the whole idea of *binding* and *loosing.*

When we refer to the bonds of holy matrimony, we are reflecting the language of Paul in 1 Corinthians 7. He in turn was employing common ethical language familiar to the Christian and Jewish communities of his day.

The language in both 1 Corinthians and in Romans evokes Jesus' words in Matthew 18:18:

Whatever you bind on earth shall be bound in heaven, and

whatever you loose on earth shall be loosed in heaven. This is ethical language describing a person's degree of obligation in a contracted matter. According to Thayer, to be *bound* in such a context is a "rabbinic idiom." It means to forbid or prohibit a person, or to declare this or that option illegal. To be *loosed* has the exact opposite meaning. According to Thayer, "the customary meaning of the rabbinic expressions [to bind or to loose] is incontestable, namely to declare forbidden or permitted and thus to impose or remove an obligation by a doctrinal decision."[6]

While the language is not as well defined in the Old Testament, the concept of being contractually bound or loosed is at least materially present. The rabbis of a later age would refine their words into the clear ethical sense with which they are used by both Jesus and Paul. Still, there is a rough Old Testament equivalent to the New Testament concept of being bound. It appears in Numbers 30:1-12. In that passage the Hebrew word *'asar* ("to bind") expresses the permanent nature of a person's oath no less than eight times.

In the Old Testament a person's word was clearly binding. One was bound to do what one had sworn to do. Only in exceptional circumstances could one's oath be declared null and void. The Hebrew word used for such loosing was the word *parar*. Within the context of Old Testament thinking, the rabbis developed their clear vocabulary for describing one's obligation to the law. And both Jesus and Paul employ this vocabulary in their teaching.

To be "bound" in the fullest biblical sense is incontestably to be under contractual obligations. To be "loosed" as in 1 Corinthians 7:27, or "freed" as in 1 Corinthians 7:39, or

"discharged" as in Romans 7:2, means to have all legal restrictions removed.

Having now seen that death discharges one from the marriage bond according to Scripture and that such a discharge
leaves a person free with respect to the issues in which he
or she was once bound, we should now consider the other
biblically stated conditions that can undo the marriage
bond. As we do so, we shall see that both logic and direct
scriptural statements sustain the fact that when a bond is
loosened, the person once under that bond becomes free.

First, we must consider the condition of repeated and unrepented sexual sin. Next, there is the consideration of a
desertion from the marital agreement. Scripture teaches
that both these conditions can fracture the marriage bond.
The Scripture also teaches that people under the obligations
of such bonds can be set free. Once these two issues are
discussed, the burning question remains—who is to decide
in such matters? Are these matters to be settled for the
Christian by the state, or by the private parties themselves
alone? Or could it be that God has another way in mind?

Repeated Sexual Sin Breaks the Marriage Bond
It is very difficult to ignore the fact that Jesus taught that
repeated sexual sin places a marriage in grave danger and
may be acceptable grounds for a divorce according to Scripture.

The passages in question are Matthew 5:32 and Matthew
19:9:

But I say to you that every one who divorces his wife,
except on the ground of unchastity, makes her an adul-

teress; and whoever marries a divorced woman commits adultery. [The Greek word translated here as *unchastity* is *porneia*. More will be said about this important word.]

And I say to you: whoever divorces his wife, except for unchastity *[porneia]*, and marries another, commits adultery.

In two more abbreviated accounts (Mk 10:11-12; Lk 16:18) the so-called exception clause is omitted.

While both Matthew 5 and Matthew 19 state exceptions to Jesus' basic doctrine of the inviolate nature of marriage, Matthew 5 uses a more distinct and emphatic expression. The Greek phrase appearing in Matthew 5, *parektos logou porneias* ("except in a matter of fornication"), is more unusual than Matthew 19's simple phrase *me epi porneia* ("except for fornication"). It seems as if the phrase in Matthew 5 were designed to invite a closer examination. And we shall do just that. Nevertheless it can be said at the outset that both passages are clear in stating that Jesus allows for the possibility of divorce if one of the marriage partners is involved in acts of fornication.

Looking closer at Matthew 5 because of its distinctive wording, we see that several things are suggested by the use of the somewhat emphatic clause "except in a matter of fornication."

First, the Greek word *fornication (porneia)*, though hotly debated in certain quarters, can at least be said to describe serious sexual sins—sexual sins which would be of the worst kind, adultery or homosexual practices for example, as opposed to flights of sexual fantasy or looking at a woman (or a man) with lust.[7]

Second, Matthew 5 seems to say that the sexual sin referred to has to be a substantiated fact. This is suggested by the words "a matter of," which probably reflect a Hebrew idiom which carries a certain legal connotation. Moreover, beyond the explicit wording, the implicit logic of the verse and the basic New Testament aversion to hearsay and unsubstantiated accusations make it all the more certain that the sexual sin referred to in the exception clause must be a clearly established fact.[8]

Third, an understanding of the New Testament teaching on forgiveness must be brought to this passage if we are to arrive at a proper Christian interpretation of it. We must understand that the sexual sin referred to in Matthew 5:32 describes a repeated transgression of which the guilty party refuses to repent. This is not simply a single indiscretion. The initial response of a Christian when offended is to forgive. Jesus says we are to forgive our brother, not seven times, but seventy times seven times (Mt 18:21-22). The only thing that cannot be forgiven is a refusal to repent.

One may not be able to argue conclusively from the language alone that the expression "a matter of fornication" refers to repeated sin, though a case could be made that the wording itself implies this.[9] Nevertheless, we should understand the intent of Matthew 5:32 in the light of Jesus' commands that his followers be forgiving. These commands abound throughout the New Testament. It is best to see only repeated and thus unrepented sexual sin as being referred to here. Jesus, in Matthew 5:32, is describing a persistent condition, not an isolated instance.

We must not be inflexible in our application of Matthew

5:32 to life situations. We should always remember that an overly scrupulous, stringently literalistic observance of Jesus' words can produce as brutal a system of legalism as that of the scribes and Pharisees which Jesus opposed so vigorously. Divorce is not to be seen as some sort of revenge visited as punishment on someone for a single, sinful act. It is rather a tragic necessity when a marriage partner continues, without repentance, to violate God's moral law.

Fourth, since Jesus says in Matthew 5:32 that repeated sexual sin is an acceptable ground for divorce, it must mean that the marriage bond is broken. If this were not the case, then we would be faced with the untenable conclusion that Jesus is encouraging people to break God's law. If the marriage bond remains intact, then Jesus would be allowing for people to "put asunder" that which God "joined together." This would be an internal contradiction incapable of a Christian defense.

Evidently the unrepentant sexual offender has broken the union. Or, to put it more precisely, if the sexual offender has committed transgressions of such a magnitude, the church may, as Jesus says in Matthew 18, exercise its authority to declare the marriage bond broken and the parties involved free or "loosed" from their marital obligations.

If he refuses to listen even to the church, let him be to you as a Gentile and a tax collector. Truly, I say to you, whatever you bind on earth shall be bound in heaven, and whatever you loose on earth shall be loosed in heaven. (Mt 18:17-18)

In reality, it appears that the sexual transgressions implied in the exception clause of Matthew 5:32 require the disso-

lution of the union. The innocent party cannot be held guilty of breaking the marital bond. If that is so, then the potential sin of adultery is also removed, because the union which a remarriage would have violated no longer exists. Adultery cannot be a potential sin where the marriage bond no longer exists. Adultery can only be charged when a marital union is in existence.

Jesus is saying that a marriage should not be disregarded when its bonds still exist. To remarry when a previous marriage remains in force would be wrong since that second marriage would transgress the first marriage bond. This would be adultery. However, if the marriage bond is declared broken because of sexual sin, that marriage bond no longer exists and there is no potential sin of adultery pending in the case of a possible remarriage. The existence or nonexistence of a marriage bond is the only logical concern in the question of remarriage. We will look at this more closely later.

Finally, we must face the fact that divorce may be a tragic necessity if a marriage partner adamantly refuses to abide by any tolerable moral standard. Unrepentant and repeated sexual transgression would make a marriage not only impossible, but—and this must be stated with caution—it would perversely turn the marriage into a form of subsidy for sin. In a very real sense, a refusal to respond to fornication by the innocent party may actually aid and abet that immorality by allowing its expression to continue unchecked. There are tragic times in the life of the Christian community when divorce is not merely allowable, it is imperative.

Consider Matthew 5:32 once more.

But I say to you that every one who divorces his wife, except on the ground of unchastity, makes her an adulteress; and whoever marries a divorced woman commits adultery.

The implications that have been drawn from this verse can be summarized as follows:

☐ The sins of Matthew 5:32 are sexual sins.

☐ The sexual sins of Matthew 5:32 must be substantiated.

☐ The substantiated, sexual sins of Matthew 5:32 are repeated and are not confessed in repentance.

☐ The repeated, unconfessed, substantiated, sexual sins of Matthew 5:32 are legitimate grounds over which the marital union may be broken.

☐ The unrepented, substantiated, sexual sins against the marital union described Matthew 5:32 must be disciplined by God's people.

As we examine this verse, our understanding of how the marriage bond can be broken—and how divorce may be possible—slowly becomes more clear.

Desertion Breaks the Marriage Bond

But there is another instance in which the marriage bond is destroyed—desertion. The critical passage concerning desertion and Christian marriage is 1 Corinthians 7:10-16 and centers around the Pauline Concession of verse 15.

If the unbelieving partner desires to separate, let it be so; in such a case the brother or sister is not bound. For God has called us to peace.

The chapter is complicated and contains several problems in understanding the apostolic teaching. There are certain fine points in any in-depth discussion of 1 Corinthians 7 which must be addressed. Among these points is the important question of the meaning of being "bound" and being "free" according to Paul, as we have already discussed. And we will return to this subject later when we address the issue of remarriage.

It may prove helpful at this point, however, to consider the passage in an overview before zeroing in on its particulars. 1 Corinthians 7 revolves around the theme of marriage and Christian family life. It was written by Paul in response to one of several questions the Corinthians posed to him in a letter (1 Cor 7:1). Paul's response to the questions of their letter comprises much of the last nine chapters of 1 Corinthians. As 7:1 indicates, the first question concerned sexual relationships and marriage. The sections that generally interest those concerned with the question of divorce are verses 1-16 and 35-40.

The following topical outline of 1 Corinthians 7 may help fit the individual arguments into a broader picture.

An Outline of 1 Corinthians 7

I. Lesson 1—On marriage, 7:1-7

Main Point: Though Paul personally prefers celibacy (vv. 1, 7), he also says "each man should have his own wife and each woman her own husband" (v. 2).

II. Lesson 2—To the *agamois* (unmarried) and widows, 7:8-9

Main Point: "It is better to marry than to be aflame with passion" (v. 9).

III. Lesson 3—On Jesus' teaching concerning marriage and

divorce, 7:10-11

Main Point: "The wife should not separate from her husband, . . . and . . . the husband should not divorce his wife" (vv. 10-11).

IV. Lesson 4—To everyone else: An extension by the apostle on Jesus' teaching on marriage and divorce, 7:12-16

Main Point: "God has called us to peace" (v. 15).

V. Lesson 5—On contentment, 7:17-24

Main Point: "So, brethren, in whatever state each was called, there let him remain with God" (v. 24).

VI. Lesson 6—Concerning the "present distress," 7:25-35

Main Point: "I want you to be free from anxieties" (v. 32).

VII. Lesson 7—Concerning engagements, 7:36-38

Main Point: "He who marries his betrothed does well; and he who refrains from marriage will do better" (v. 38).

VIII. Final Words—7:39-40

Main Point: "A wife is bound to her husband. . . . If the husband dies, she is free to be married . . . in the Lord" (v. 39).

As the outline shows, Paul's words in 7:12-16 addressing everyone else ("the rest") should be seen as the apostle extending Jesus' basic teaching into other areas. When he says "I say, not the Lord," he is simply stating the obvious. Jesus, in his ministry on earth, did not comment on all the possible complexities that may surround marital problems. Paul wants to consider one such issue, the issue of desertion.

Unless we are seeking to fragment the authority of Scripture and start an insane and subjective process by which we will ultimately choose what Scripture we will obey and what Scripture we will not obey, then we must acknowledge that

Paul's words are as authoritative as any other Scripture. If we are to be in any sense spiritual, we will acknowledge that Paul has God's Holy Spirit (1 Cor 7:40) and that he is delivering a command of the Lord's (1 Cor 14:37). Paul's word is as binding as all other Scripture. To think otherwise is to court destruction.[10]

The teaching within Paul's concession (1 Cor 7:15) concerning the desertion of a marriage partner by his or her mate is fairly straightforward. One is tempted to wonder whether the apostle would be surprised at the myriad of inventive interpretations of his words which he expressed so briefly and concisely. While I have no wish to add to this creative parade, a few brief observations are in order. More will be said about this critical passage later.

Paul identifies the one who abandons a marriage partner as an unbeliever. This decision is serious and is presumed to be done by the church in keeping with Jesus' instruction that unrepentant offenders are to be regarded as unbelievers. "If he refuses to listen even to the church, let him be to you as a Gentile and a tax collector" (Mt 18:17).

It is not inconceivable that a Christian would sin. In fact, it should be a foregone conclusion that Christians will sin. The mark of a Christian is not sinlessness but rather sorrow for sin.

What is inconceivable is that a believer who has committed a clear act of immorality should persist not only in that sin but also in a refusal to admit the sin and repent of it. For someone to call himself or herself a Christian and yet refuse to be reconciled to an innocent mate and simply walk away from a marriage is difficult to understand. Scripture teaches that Christians possess the Holy Spirit and have become "new creatures" in Christ—and this should be reflected in our attitudes toward reconciliation.

It is not a Christian's wrongdoing that is surprising, it is his or her conscious persistence in moral sin. The perseverance in moral sin and the refusal to call it sin is difficult to reconcile with a profession of faith. This is why Paul says what he does in 1 Corinthians 6:9-10.

> Do you not know that the unrighteous will not inherit the kingdom of God? Do not be deceived; neither the immoral, nor idolaters, nor adulterers, nor sexual perverts, nor thieves, nor the greedy, nor drunkards, nor revilers, nor robbers will inherit the kingdom of God.

It is not so much the case that Christians are incapable of lapses into such behavior; no, Christians certainly possess the ability to sin. It is clearly the teaching of this and other passages[11] that Christians do not persist in such behavior without "coming to themselves" and repenting. Certainly the final judgment on whether or not a particular individual is a believer is for God to make. However, in cases of moral decisions, those in church leadership must be prepared to move on the assumption that the unrepentant sinner, even though he calls himself a believer, is not to be regarded as a believer. It is a very dangerous thing to regard those who persist in moral sin as simply "backsliding" Christians. For one thing, it is a violation of direct scriptural teaching:

> I wrote to you not to associate with any one who bears the name of brother if he is guilty of immorality or greed, or is an idolater, reviler, drunkard, or robber—not even to eat with such a one. For what have I to do with judging

outsiders? Is it not those inside the church whom you are to judge? God judges those outside. "Drive out the wicked person from among you." (1 Cor 5:11-13)

If we mistakenly allow ourselves to believe that Paul would place some people into a separate category of "Christians," designed for those who claim to have faith in Christ and yet abandon their mates and prove false to their most sacred promise, we would be making a catastrophic error. Christians do not do things like that. And, though God is always the final judge, leaders in the church would be seriously in default if they called people "Christians" who behave this way. It would be antinomianism to do that. Christians mustn't think they can sweep any immoral behavior under a tattered rug of assumed privilege, freedom and easy forgiveness simply because they have received salvation. Some may think that the gospel allows them to break God's moral law with impunity. They are wrong.

As we saw in Matthew 5, the church is to take an active role in the resolution of conflict. This is Paul's strong conviction within the Corinthian letter.

Do you not know that we are to judge angels? How much more, matters pertaining to this life! If then you have such cases, why do you lay them before those who are least esteemed by the church? I say this to your shame. Can it be that there is no man among you wise enough to decide between members of the brotherhood? (1 Cor 6:3-5)

The breakdown of a marriage must be regarded as the ultimate in human conflict. Certainly the church must be active in bringing moral judgment and just resolution to the tragedies of divorce.

44

So-called Christians who behave continually like pagans have no assurance that they are anything *but* pagans. The church must affirm this. An unbeliever is as an unbeliever does. The Scripture is consistently clear on this.

Anyone who abandons his or her filial obligations, for example, is "worse than an unbeliever" (1 Tim 5:8). And, as we have seen above, we are warned not even to associate with immoral persons who presume to the title of "brother" (1 Cor 5:11). Who is to make such determinations? According to Scripture, it is the local church body. The local church is a pattern of authority in the Christian life that must take an active role in the resolution of conflict and moral confusion in the life of God's people. A degree of sanctified cynicism would well be directed toward the person who can so casually desert his or her spouse and at the same time glibly profess faith in God. "Oh, you believe in God, do you? That's just fine! So does the devil" (to paraphrase James 2:19).

Paul goes on to note that the marital deserter is viewed as an unbeliever. It would be inconceivable to Paul that Christians would be guilty of deserting their marriage vows. However, it should be noted that desertion can be extremely subtle. If we are not careful and define desertion as only a physical distancing of two bodies, we are liable to turn a deaf ear to an incredible amount of intolerable physical and emotional abuse that takes place under the same roof. Togetherness is not an ideal in itself—the respectful and obedient fulfillment of covenant promises before God is.

Desertion can mean more than mere physical relocation.

A wife once sat in my office and insisted that divorce was out of the question, even though her adulterous husband was being physically abusive to her and homosexually assaulting their adopted preadolescent child. Though he was guilty of horrible abuse, she correctly pointed out that he had not physically deserted the home. With the help of a lawyer, in spite of the woman's reluctance, the church pressed to achieve some semblance of moral order in this awful situation. The man was "persuaded" to allow the child to be removed from his home by a social agency. The prospect of a long prison term was most persuasive in his thinking.

Persistent behavior such as this is desertion. It is a flagrant abandonment of all the responsibilities of a husband and father's sacred duties before God. I do not believe that God is calling us to the kind of torturous ethical gyrations that would have the man thrown in prison so that the wife could hit him with Paul's concession and divorce him for desertion.

If the unbeliever departs, Paul counsels the believer to "let it be." Clearly this has a logical connection to the peace that is to characterize the final disposition of the Christian heart. As we have already said, if the church, in keeping with its prerogative to adjudicate in moral conflict, pronounces a person not to be bound, then that person is not bound. And, unless we succumb to games of pure sophistry and word-wars, to be pronounced *free* is to be free to marry again. "Only," as Paul counsels in 1 Corinthians 7:39, "marry in the Lord."

Although there is more to consider on the question of 1 Corinthians 7, we will let these last few comments suffice for the moment.

In this chapter of Scripture, desertion does not carry with it the moral imperative of divorce that the immorality of

Matthew 5:32 does. However, desertion and the failure of the one who deserts to provide proper support for children's emotional and physical needs are bound together. This may make divorce in the case of a desertion a moral imperative.

Welfare assistance, for example, is often denied if the applicant is legally married. If the undefined legal status of an abandoned spouse interferes with that spouse securing the proper assistance from the church or the state to meet the needs of dependent children, then divorce becomes morally imperative in the case of desertion.

In the matter of serious moral problems, the local church must be active in bringing judgment and justice to the issues as they involve believers. It would be hard to deny that those who are facing the disruption of their marriages are experiencing serious moral problems. It follows quite logically that the local church must be involved in the resolution of such problems. The local church must be ready to make hard decisions and take courageous stands. To allow individual Christians to make final authoritative decisions in these matters on their own moral recognizance, as it were, is foreign to any biblical ethical system. It is also unfair. Believers caught up in such difficulties are in the most vulnerable of positions. The local church must be there for them.

As with many other matters in 1 Corinthians, the implicit need to judge in a situation such as desertion is assumed to be the prerogative of the local church. As we have seen, Paul makes this abundantly clear in 1 Corinthians 5:9—6:8. The local church must come to the aid of those of its number who are in moral difficulty. We are not to stand alone, decide alone and endure alone in matters of divorce and remarriage.

The Local Church Must Be Involved

Christians must acknowledge the unique role of the church to adjudge the facts of such situations. Biblical order and morality must be maintained within the fellowship of the local church. In resolving conflicts between Christians, Jesus commanded his church to follow a pattern of attempted reconciliation. Sadly, the matter of divorce in the church is an all-too-familiar example of conflict between Christians.

The biblical process for resolving conflict is fairly straightforward:

> If your brother sins against you, go and tell him his fault, between you and him alone. If he listens to you, you have gained your brother. But if he does not listen, take one or two others along with you, that every word may be confirmed by the evidence of two or three witnesses. If he refuses to listen to them, tell it to the church; and if he refuses to listen even to the church, let him be to you as a Gentile and a tax collector. Truly, I say to you, whatever you bind on earth shall be bound in heaven, and whatever you loose on earth shall be loosed in heaven. Again I say to you, if two of you agree on earth about anything they ask, it will be done for them by my Father in heaven. For where two or three are gathered in my name, there am I in the midst of them. (Mt 18:15–20)

Personal attempts to reconcile differences must be made. At a second level, two or three others are brought in for clarity, and finally, if a sinning party remains unrepentant, we must "tell it to the church." And if he or she refuses to listen even to the church, we must let that person be the same as an unbeliever in our eyes. Such judgments are the ultimate province of the church. The local church, for discipline and purity's sake, must declare the judgment of heaven in issues that dissolve marital unions on earth.

Discernment and judgment are required. Arriving at the conclusion that a divorce is permissible was never intended by the New Testament to be the prerogative of any one person, let alone the person who is being seriously stressed by the moral matter in question. Such questions as who is the guilty party in a divorce, or who is or is not a Christian, are questions for the church to decide. Contrary to popular practice in the church today, everyone is not to do what is right in his or her own eyes.

The Issue of Remarriage

As we have seen, Paul states that a Christian is no longer "bound" to a spouse who departs and refuses to honor the moral conditions of a marriage vow. This is stated expressly in 1 Corinthians 7. We have also seen that a similar release from the bond of matrimony is the implicit teaching of Jesus in Matthew 5:32 and 19:9. The departing spouse, like the sexually immoral spouse, has been proven to be an unbelieving, irreconcilable mate.

When the bond of marriage has been effectively "loosed," the possibility of a remarriage cannot be denied.

One may well observe that the explicit command of 1 Corinthians 7:11 prohibits remarriage. "Let [them] remain single or else be reconciled to [their mates]." This is undeniably true and must be considered absolutely binding *as long as the possibility of reconciliation remains.*

But obviously there comes a time when it must be determined that reconciliation is no longer an option.

This is the case when one of the parties remarries or plunges into unbridled sexual sin. But, it is also subtly the case when the irreconcilable mate remains adamantly separate. The possibility of remarriage must be considered if for no other reason than the teaching of 1 Corinthians 7:9: "It is better to marry than to be aflame with passion."

This concern was first voiced by Jesus in his observation that not all men can "receive" the imposition of enforced celibacy.[12] Paul seems to be expounding on that consideration at the outset of his discussion in 1 Corinthians 7 when he makes it clear that the conjugal needs of married partners must be given serious consideration (1 Cor 7:3). Furthermore, Paul states that the deprivation of a sexual partner is not spiritually wise, according to 1 Corinthians 7:5. The imposition of celibacy on a mate who is not guilty of deserting his or her marriage is inconsistent with all of what Scripture has to say on the subject.

But if remarriage is possible in the case of desertion, who is to determine this? As in all such sensitive matters of moral discernment, the local church is God's instrument in the making of difficult moral judgments.

In the case of desertion in 1 Corinthians 7, the faithful, believing party may be judged as no longer bound since God has called believers to peace (1 Cor 7:15).

As noted earlier, the language in 1 Corinthians 7 is the language of moral obligation. To be "bound" is to be committed to all the moral obligations of a given agreement. To be "bound" in marriage is to be liable to uphold all the requirements that the Bible exacts from those who are in the bonds of holy matrimony. To break that bond would be an illicit act.

However, if a person is no longer bound in marriage, then he or she must be regarded as free from any prohibitions concerning marriage. Paul declares this in 1 Corinthians 7:15:

> But if the unbelieving partner desires to separate, let it be so; in such a case the brother or sister *is not bound.* For God has called us to peace. [emphasis mine]

Some argue that the phrase "not bound" in 1 Corinthians 7:15 refers only to the past marriage. They insist that the phrase carries no significance for the possibility of remarriage after the divorce. But to interpret the phrase "not bound" in 1 Corinthians 7:15 in any other light than that it means to be set free from what is prohibited to those who are bound would be both a defiance of logic and language, as well as a denial of sound interpretive principles.

To insist that the phrase "not bound" does not allow for the possibility of remarriage is to argue from something more than the text itself. Such an insistence reads far more into the phrase in terms of prohibition than is required or even expected. If it were not for the extreme sensitivity of the question, the phrase "not bound" would hardly be seen as anything other than a declaration permitting remarriage, since the whole idea of being bound in marriage means to be bound *to* a specific person and *from* marriage to any other person.

If, as Paul says in 1 Corinthians 7, there is no more bondage but only peace, then it follows that the *actual* sin of divorce, that of breaking a God-ordained union, has not been committed by the innocent party. The binding union, fractured by the deserting party, may be judged by the church as no longer in force. Now if the union no longer exists, it follows that the *potential* sin of divorce, that of adultery, must no longer be seen as an issue, since adultery can only be a violation of an existing union. Paul speaks to this in 1 Corinthians 7:27-28 as well:

> Are you bound to a wife? [That is, are you married?] Do not seek to be free. Are you free from a wife? Do not seek marriage. But if you marry, you do not sin.

To be "free from a wife" (literally "loosed") is not merely to be a bachelor. For several reasons it can be shown that it means "no longer married."

First, the context places the idea of freedom next to that of being presently bound in marriage. The implication is that something more than celibacy is the focus here.

Second, for Paul to use the familiar ethical idiom "loosed" with regard to marriage implies a previous marriage for the one who is now loosed. One is loosed from something. Paul would not refer to someone as "free" when he or she had never been "bound" in the first place.

Finally, the verb tense of the phrase "are you free" (v. 27) indicates a condition begun at a point in the past with continuing results. It is the Greek perfect tense. It may be literally translated "have you been loosed?" Such an expression calls for the understanding that previously there had been a binding situation and now, in its place, there is a "loosing."[13]

The major objection to remarriage after divorce is the question of adultery. However, if the marital union is broken as Scripture acknowledges it can be, then the potential concern over adultery is no longer a factor.

It is true that we should not seek to sever what God has joined. However from the words of Jesus and Paul we realize that there are times when it becomes necessary, by the authority of the local church, to end a marriage. If, as Paul says, a believer is no longer bound in such cases, then remarriage is certainly an option.

Remarriage is never commanded. In fact, it may not be the wisest course for certain divorced people to pursue. Nevertheless, one is forced to conclude that every scripturally valid ground for breaking the bond of matrimony (whether death, sexual sin or desertion) provides a valid scriptural ground for remarriage. This is clear from the implicit logic of God's Word as well as explicit biblical teaching.

The Sins of the Past
The realities of a true and honest conversion to Christ render the sins of the past inoperative on the present (2 Cor 5:17; Gal 2:20). Consequently, pre-Christian divorce and remarriage must be dealt with by the realities of the cross. If reconciliation with the former spouse is rendered impossible by a second marriage, or other judged complications, the new believer should consider his or her past liabilities to be assumed by the Lord at the cross. This too, however, requires the healing touch of the local church's involvement.

As with all matters of moral complexity (a concern that will be addressed in the next chapter), the issues of divorce

and remarriage of believers should fall under the discipline
and protection of a local church. The issues surrounding the
divorced and remarried and their tasks in the church are
highly complex and call for the highest standards among
church leadership involving good judgment, sound biblical
knowledge, as well as a sensitive and discrete attitude. Ow-
ing to the complexities of modern life these questions must
be dealt with carefully by the church from a position of
strength, confidence, balanced judgment and a complete re-
liance on the Spirit of Christ in our midst.

It has been my experience, after nearly two decades of
pastoral ministry, that like the proverbial monkey at the
typewriter punching out infinite combinations of words,
there are an infinite number of human situations which color
the issues of marriage and divorce. Such diversity makes
simple answers dangerous.

When I was younger, the issues of marriage and divorce
seemed clear and simple. They were as uncluttered by complexity as my thinking was by experience. In those days it
was my opinion that such problems were better faced with
courageous conviction, not soul-searching deliberation. It
was my firm conviction that believers never married unbelievers, period. Divorce was never right, period. And remarriage after a divorce was wrong, period. A few ironclad principles answered the whole gamut of possible human
situations. Such was my naiveté. But I hope the church will
be governed by more mature thinking.

The Big Leagues
I had a friend in high school. We played football together. As

befitted our respective athletic abilities, I went into the pastorate and he went into the NFL. My friend has probably played in more Super Bowl games than almost anyone.

He was drafted by the Green Bay Packers. And when they stopped winning everything in sight, he was traded to Miami. This was about the time the Dolphins began the only undefeated season in the modern NFL.

I mention my friend because of the particular story he once told me about his rookie year. In a preseason exhibition game Bart Star sent him down on a decoy pass pattern. That is, he was to go out as if he were going to catch a pass when in fact the quarterback had no intention of throwing it to him. He was a decoy. It can fool the defense if it is run with a good deal of effort and theatrics.

But my friend was tired and definitely not feeling "theatrical." With little or no conviction, he jogged through his fake-pass route. Head down, disinterested . . . poor theater.

It was on that particular day that he met one of the finest linebackers in the league. Or at least he met his forearm—across the neck. It's called a "clothesline," named after that treacherous little stretch of cord on which you hang your laundry and which under no circumstances should ever be encountered unknowingly, at neck level, while running in the dark. If executed properly, the "clothesline" could be an execution.

It was executed very well. My friend couldn't talk for a week.

As he lay gasping on his back, the whistle blew. The linebacker (who shall remain nameless) trotted past my friend who lay purple and wheezing on the turf. Evidently, the linebacker had not appreciated my friend's lackadaisical pass pattern. Perhaps the linebacker felt it showed a lack of respect for his territory, or some primal concern like that.

He snarled down to him: "This is pro football, rookie."

I share the story because it captures my own feelings after my first few months as a "rookie" pastor. Sitting confused and numb at my desk, at times I swear I could almost hear someone taunting me: "This is the ministry, rookie."

Bill, Jane and the Witch

I was fresh from seminary, ready to minister and full of the right answers to all the important questions. I eagerly faced the prospect of caring for, counseling and teaching people in the midst of their daily lives. Above all other thorny problems, I knew for whom I would and would not perform a marriage ceremony. The purity of my church would remain unsullied.

Armed with this strong conviction and untempered ideal, I encountered my first request to marry a couple. I soon learned many things, not the least being that God must have a sense of humor.

I'll call him Bill. He was a small businessman who traded on the fringes of our university town's youth culture. He had sowed more wild oats than Quaker could supply and wasn't through farming yet. He had, however, met a young woman eight years prior whom I'll call Jane. He was deeply attached to her.

For more than seven years they had lived together, as we say so delicately, without benefit of clergy. In our particular state there was no such thing as common-law marriage, so their relationship remained unsanctioned by the state—not to mention unsanctified by any church.

Bill found that life in the fast lane was full of painful collisions with reality. One day he woke up to find that his "roommate" had skipped town with a serviceman who was passing through.

Bill took it hard. He felt he needed some good advice, advice from a higher power. For the first time in his life he sought spiritual help. Unfortunately, he consulted a witch.

Don't laugh! North Florida abounds with soothsayers, palm readers, mystic advisors and any number of covens. Evidently it's part of the cultural tradition.

Bill's encounter with this "spiritual advisor" nearly frightened him to death. Not only was he taken for over one hundred dollars, but this worldly wise businessman was willing to spend it, just so long as he didn't have to deal with that witch again. It was a bad trip, as they used to say in the late sixties. A real bummer.

Bill, who had never thought much about God, was now convinced there was a devil. He began to wonder about God too. And as he wondered about these things he longed for Jane to return.

About this time a member of our fellowship invited Bill to dinner. Lonely and confused, Bill came, and in the course of the evening got it all off his chest. He missed his girl. He desperately wanted her to come back to him. And now he was scared about spiritual things too. Who was God? Could God help him? At dinner that night, Bill heard the gospel and called on the Lord Jesus to save him.

I was introduced to Bill through his new Christian friends.

From almost the first minute we met, Bill began to recite what was to become nearly a litany with him: "Pastor, I'm asking God to bring Jane back to me. And if he does, I want to make an honest woman of her."

"Pastor," he asked with large and innocent eyes, "will you marry us if God answers my prayer?"

Although still a novice, I was already learning appropriate non sequiturs—the double-talk-but-be-spiritual avoidance ploy. Doing a fine imitation of Ted Baxter, the incredibly inept newscaster on the old "Mary Tyler Moore Show," ("Take off glasses, look concerned," Ted once solemnly intoned as he mistakenly read the parenthetic stage directions along with the news copy off Mary's cue cards), I said, "Bill, I'm going to join you in that prayer."

Unfortunately, God answered Bill's prayer.

Jane returned. She was thoroughly repentant, thrilled at the possibility of marriage and willing to consider the relevance of Bill's newfound faith. But she was not ready to make a commitment, though she was intrigued by it all.

From the knock on my study door I knew it was Bill. And I knew what he wanted. Since his fiancée returned, they had remained chaste for each other. It was not easy. The old patterns ran deep and their desire to be together was strong. But he didn't want to sin. He wanted to make an honest woman out of her.

Jane, on the other hand, was not ready to embrace the faith. I was profoundly uneasy about coercing her into a profession of faith. I knew she needed to honestly repent. I wanted to say, "Sorry, I don't marry Christians to non-Christians!" But I didn't say anything.

In quiet desperation, I sought the help of the oldest, most experienced pastors in our district. I talked with some of my former seminary professors. And I talked the matter over at length with the elders of our church.

It was unanimous: they all said I should go ahead and marry this Christian to a non-Christian. It was something that I swore I would never do. It was contrary to the general principles of Scripture. It was an unequal partnership between a Christian and a non-Christian (2 Cor 6:14).

It was my first wedding as a new pastor.

Bill got a wife. She got a husband, and later made a profession of faith. I got . . . confused!

My ideals got the edges knocked off them, and I discovered that life is not a text book. . . . It is a maze of complexities.

I began to learn that God's absolute and unalterable law, his moral law, is not to be used as if it were a set of directions printed inside a put-it-together-yourself swing set. ("Connect rod *A* to the double-lined flange protector . . . or die!")

No, God's Word is alive, quick and powerful, and meant to be used in living situations to bring life and hope into the wilderness of human rebellion and misery. I also learned that, for pompous young seminary students like me who had reality neatly categorized and packaged (and who knew just who can and who can't get married), God in his infinite mercy does have a sense of humor.

Morality and Shades of Gray
Perhaps I should hasten to add that I am not one-hundred

per-cent sure I did the right thing here. Clearly I had to do something, and no story in itself should be regarded as a paradigm for right behavior. The ends never justify the means. I am prepared to defend my action as pastor, and our elders are prepared to defend their part in the decision. And one day we will do just that when we stand before God.

Now, in the light of the serious consequences of our decision, one might be tempted to say that making *no* decision is the best solution. Yes—if you are just trying to cover yourself in life, and remain intent on not getting involved, this may seem the safest route. But avoiding moral risks is not the same as achieving moral safety.

Refusing to get involved is not the route of the good Samaritan whom Jesus held up to us as a moral guide. If we are going to help people, taking risks is a must. Groping in uncertain darkness at times is unavoidable. After all, many people live in that darkness. Avoiding risky and questionable moral decisions is not merely moral cowardice, it is moral devastation in the lives of those who look to the church for guidance in the thorny questions of life.

I shared this story for one primary reason. I wanted to make the point that moral matters can be complex. Casting hard-and-fast principles in the concrete of certainty without reckoning with subtleties of meaning is unwise. Christians committed to biblical truth must not espouse situational ethics, but there is no such thing as an ethic without a situation. Our principles must be open to life. No, our principles should not be blown about by the winds of circumstance, but certainly they should be flexible and interactive in order to discern another kind of wind—the promptings of the Holy

Spirit. Our moral convictions are not merely bastions of truth to keep the ungodly from our midst. On the contrary, our convictions and principles must form islands of rest and refuge for those seeking shelter in the inevitable times when moral storms blow across our lives.

3
Facing the Complexities of Life

*O*ne of the major obstacles in defining the role of divorced people in the church is the Gordian knot of life situations and problems which surround even the most simple cases of divorce. Life can be extremely complex. Our motivations can often be ambiguous and ambivalent even to ourselves.

Beyond that, others may perceive what we do and say far differently from what we intend. And though these perceptions may differ sharply with our own, they may honestly be held by those who disagree with us.

We must add to that matrix of complexity the universal solvent of time. Time blends and blurs our acts and intentions in our own mind as well as in the minds of others. It becomes quite possible for one person to remember (or think he remembers) something quite different from what really happened. Often this blurring-by-time is not an intentional alteration but the operation of distance on natural human frailty. As a result of these and many other factors, life situations can become extremely complex.

This must be reckoned with whenever human situations are addressed and human problems dealt with in counseling. Biblical healing and spiritual counsel require both empathy and compassion. Too often evangelicals are quick to label the "bad guy" and lower the boom on the "guilty party." But disagreements, even sharp and heated ones, do not mean that one party is lying.

I recall walking out of a Christian meeting one evening with a friend of mine and being handed a particular pamphlet. It looked just like the material that had been passed out in the meeting that evening. However, this pamphlet was not put out by the sponsors of that meeting. In fact, the material we were given as we left was a challenge to many of the things we had heard inside. Even though the pamphlet took issue with the meeting, it had been purposely disguised to appear to be part of the official papers of the proceedings that had just concluded. To be sure, this was a highly unethical thing to do.

My friend took one look at the material and said, "Well, this is certainly of the devil." I asked him (politely, I hope) how he knew it was "of the devil."

He seemed surprised at my question. Referring to the shoddy ethics behind the distribution of the pamphlet, he said, "Well, it sure wasn't of God, was it?"

I assured him that I didn't think it was, and that I too thought it unethical. But it seemed to me that there were a number of other wills in the universe beside God's and the devil's.

You see, things aren't always so simple. We may long to brand this act or that opinion as devilish. It does make things simpler. One should never argue with the devil, after all. Unfortunately, human situations are more complex than that.

This is paramountly true regarding issues surrounding marriage and divorce. I have rarely found a "good guy" and a "bad guy." The intimate relationship of a man and wife is very complex, and the issues involved demand the utmost patience, wisdom and love.

The Need for Judgment in Complex Situations

The questions concerning the role of the divorced and remarried in the church fall headlong into this inevitable human cycle of confusion and uncertainty. Those desiring biblical behavior and moral answers in these areas are often confused by the complexities of life. Nevertheless, all moral problems and moral solutions fall into this tempestuous sea and can often be swirled about until, after a time, many moral situations calling for moral responses seem a hopeless tangle at very best.

What is to be done? The temptation to do nothing is great. To some, in the face of such complexity, a simple, inflexible rule or prohibition applied to all situations of divorce equally and impartially is the only answer. Unfortunately it is not a biblical answer.

Certainly a retreat from decision in the face of complexity is a moral failure of nerve. It lacks courage. As Christians we care very deeply about the moral issues of life. And so we should! We love God. And we have been loved by God and forgiven for our own moral failures. Christians can never be indifferent to the moral matters of life again. As a result, hopefully, perhaps idealistically and sometimes naively, we attempt to confront the moral complexities of life with the answers of the gospel.

We understand the gospel fairly well, and the Scriptures are not totally foreign to us, but as we mature we find life growing increasingly complex and confusing. As Christians we may then long for the simple answer and the "easy fix." But the more God grants us insights into life, the more we realize that simple, moralistic answers are unsatisfactory. In fact, they may possibly be even more destructive than the moral problems they purport to solve.

Linda and the Love of God

Linda wasn't born in this country. And of course "Linda" isn't her real name—but you have to start somewhere. It gets kind of confusing.

Linda met her husband Bob while he was on duty with the armed forces in her native country. They were married and, after Bob's tour was up, they headed back to this country. Linda said goodbye to her family and set off to explore a land she'd never seen and live in a culture that was strange and foreign to her. Her English was so slight, it was nearly non-existent.

Shortly after they arrived, Linda got a job. She worked in a factory. The hours were tolerable and the pay was more than she ever dreamed of making. Linda, like most of her people, worked hard.

Bob's was a slightly different story.

Bob seemed to have chronic back problems. Illnesses plagued him, usually just after he got a new job. The longest job Bob managed to hold down was as a night attendant at a filling station on the interstate. But he didn't hold it down long. After a month or so Bob's boss, who had tolerated the continual lateness, had to let Bob go after he simply didn't show up for work two or three nights in a row.

Bob had problems. Of course Bob's problems were also Linda's and they were a long way from being over when I met them.

They had been attending our church sporadically for a while. They sat in the back, left early and quickly. I first noticed them when Bob handed in a registration card on which he said he wished the church would sing some more contemporary hymns. He suggested James Taylor's "You've Got a Friend" and another popular song of the day that had a refrain, "There ain't no good guys, there ain't no bad guys, there's only you and me, and we just disagree."

I filed the note away and thought of singing them on Reformation Sunday.

His note did get my attention. I knew their names now, and I was able to call them by name when I got the rare opportunity between the last hymn and the car door.

One day Bob called me. Could he and his wife come and talk over a problem?

Sure. And in they came.

"It's not our problem, really," Bob began. "You see my sister and her husband have been living with us for the last month—them and their three kids."

Bob told me the rest. It seems that both he and his brother-in-law were out of work. Of course Bob's sister couldn't work, with three kids and all. Linda, the only one with a job, was supporting all seven of them.

"But that's not the problem," Bob said. I was surprised to hear it wasn't. "No, the problem is that my sister has been coming to church with us lately and is feeling very guilty. You see, she was married before. She left her first husband. But now she thinks God wants her to leave her new husband, take one of the kids and go back to her ex."

"Why just one of the kids?" (I had to ask that, didn't I?)

Bob unfolded the whole crazy-quilt affair.

(As I live and breathe, what I am about to tell you is the absolute truth.) It seems there were three brothers living in a state about seven hundred miles from us. Bob's sister married the oldest brother and had a child by him. After three years of marriage, she had an affair and a child by the second brother!

After the whole thing blew apart and the inevitable divorce was decreed, Bob's sister married—you guessed it— the third brother. And she had a third son, this one by the third brother, who was her present husband.

Bob said that his sister felt she was living in a continual state of adultery and wanted to set it right. So she was thinking of leaving her second husband and taking her one son, the first husband's son, and returning to the purity of her first blessed union.

Of course all of this was wreaking additional havoc on an already chaotic domestic situation. Linda, the sole breadwinner, sat quietly while her husband spoke.

"Pastor," Bob said, "will you talk with my sister? Somehow this whole thing just doesn't seem right."

I complimented Bob on his perception. Yes, I would talk with her.

A few sessions with Bob's sister and I think we had worked out the fact that her simple solution wasn't going to work. But the worst was yet to come.

One night I got a call from the police. There had been a real knock-down, drag-out family squabble. Could I come over and help calm things down? The husband seemed desperate and was asking for me. It was Bob.

Linda had had it when she came home from work to find the three adults watching TV, and Bob's sister had asked her when dinner was going to be ready. It seems she was hungry.

In Linda's country patience was a great virtue, but so was revenge. Knife in hand, she had barely missed dispatching at least one of the three before being subdued.

My next efforts were in extracting Bob's sister, her unemployed husband and their three kids from this sagging family situation. The details of that form another episode nearly as incredible as this, but time and my sanity restrain me. Suffice it to say that they were finally helped out of Bob's home into a job and a decent rental house of their own.

But the story doesn't end here. I got another phone call. Did I know what had just happened at Bob and Linda's, a neighbor inquired. "No," I said tentatively, being fairly certain I did not want to know. "Bob just tried to kill himself. The ambulance is here. And I don't know what Linda's going to do."

Well, neither did I, but pastors aren't allowed to say that, are they?

When I got there Bob and the paramedics were gone. Linda was sitting in the front room with a dazed look. I'm not sure she understood what they had told her. Bob had slashed his wrists in their bedroom while Linda was at work. He was talking to the Suicide and Crisis Prevention Center hotline while he did it.

Usually, they say, people who attempt suicide in this manner really don't want to die. Usually. Whatever the truth in this situation, because of unclear communication and other variables, Bob came within a hair's breadth of death.

His blood covered the bedroom floor like a newly laid carpet. Linda and I went to the hospital. Bob was going to make it. It was difficult explaining the details to Linda, but eventually she understood that her husband was resting comfortably and was out of danger. He was going to be detained first for medical reasons and later for psychological reasons. Linda would be better off getting a good night's sleep and coming back tomorrow. Eventually, she agreed.

Bob had protested all along that he was a Christian. I had my doubts. As is often the case, I felt time would tell.

Linda, on the other hand, was a nominal Buddhist. The language barrier had made witnessing difficult. We had hoped that our concern as a fellowship would help over-come the obstacles.

Linda wanted to go home. I knew the state of their bed-room and tried to encourage her to spend the night in a motel. The church would take care of it. No, she wanted to go home. It meant a late-night cleaning job for me, of the most trying kind. God's grace was literally overpowering as I mopped and prayed. That too, is another story.

I'll always remember the final event of that night. I sat with Linda and carefully began to share the gospel with her as directly as the language barrier would allow. "Linda," I said, "do you know that God loves you?"

She looked at me with an open and slightly surprised look. "No," she said, "I did not know that."

There's not much more to tell. Shortly afterward both Bob and Linda left town. Only God knows the rest of the story. I share it for one reason. This is the situation that God has used most powerfully in my life to show me that life can be incredibly complex.

In the healing of hearts with the gospel of Jesus Christ there is no escaping the fact that confusion and frustration, even fear, is the inevitable price to be paid by the Lord's servants. It's best to realize this from the outset. It saves a lot of time and a lot of grief.

But for those who are courageous enough to trust the Lord and follow his pattern in solving the complex problems of life there are happy endings.

Mary's Story: When God Gets Your Attention
The farmer told the buyer when he sold him the mule that

it was perfectly trained and ready to work.

A day later the disgruntled customer returned. "Dadburn mule won't do a thing I ask it!" was the customer's far-from-patient observation. "I want my money back. You said this here mule was trained."

With little animation, the farmer shuffled slowly up to the mule and gave it a simple command. No response. The mule was regal in its impassivity—eyes disdainfully shut, jaw set and nose in the air.

The customer jeered, "See? You said he was perfectly trained. I want my money back!"

Quick as a flash, the farmer whipped out a baseball bat and, the S.P.C.A. notwithstanding, hit that mule right between the eyes. The mule obeyed the farmer's command instantly.

The customer was aghast. "What'd ya do that fer? You said that mule was trained."

" 'Course he's trained," the farmer shot back. "Ya just gotta get his attention first."

Sound familiar? I guess we all make asses out of ourselves from time to time, especially when we disobey God. And sometimes, I guess, God just has to get our attention.

Maybe that's what happened to Mary. Mary grew up in a quiet southern town. Her parents were respectable church-going people. So Mary was a churchgoer too. It was a good church where she heard the gospel and trusted Christ at an early age.

Mary was a quiet girl with many friends. She seemed to do the right thing instinctively. She rarely gave her parents trouble. And after high school, she headed off to college.

In college as in high school, Mary remained a nice, friendly person who gave little problem to anyone. The college she chose was a nominally Christian one—church-affiliated, dignified and moderate in every way. It seemed to suit Mary perfectly.

Moderation and affability, friendliness and the avoidance of excess are admirable characteristics in life, but hardly the passionate dynamics that should fuel a walk with God. We are not commanded to love God moderately. Moderation seldom engulfs all of our hearts, souls and minds.

Mary's Christian life, which had never really been nurtured, seemed to lie dormant in the attractive setting of her idyllic campus life. Studies and friends, social activities and service clubs all had a ring of reality to them that a walk with God never quite seemed to have. The Lord soon had little or no relevance as far as Mary could see.

At the end of her senior year, in the late spring, amid blossoms and bouquets, Mary wed her college sweetheart. It was, of course, a church wedding. Mary's new husband had a military obligation to fulfill, so full of newly wedded excitement, they headed off to Europe. What could possibly be more enchanting?

From this point on, Mary is not all that certain about what went wrong. Was it the shock of a different culture? Was it the upheaval of married life, so intense and personal after the distant affability of single life in the serenity of a small college campus? Or was it just a sinful, rebellious heart that lies within the breast of even the most moderate of us all?

After two years of marriage, Mary just didn't want to be

married anymore. And there didn't seem to be anything within her telling her that she should stay faithful to the man she promised to love until the parting of death. Mary walked away from her husband and that was the end of that.

By this time Mary was working at a good job, she was well supported and, being an attractive young woman living in a close community of Americans abroad, her social life was fairly active. Her old marriage faded away and a new, bright and exciting world opened up. As far as Mary was concerned, she was at the top of the world, and God was nowhere in sight.

Sometimes, I guess, God just has to get your attention. So he spoke to Mary very directly and with painful clarity.

Mary took vacation time from her work and, with a young man she was on the verge of falling in love with, set out on a winter holiday. Somewhere in the Italian Alps, Mary's happy, balanced world went spinning off into oblivion.

It happened quickly. One minute Mary and her boyfriend were speeding along a mountain road, the next minute they were careening out of control and then shooting out over the edge of the world. No one should have survived the awful crash. Mary's boyfriend didn't. And, for a long time, no one was certain that Mary would. In the pain and loss, there were times when Mary was not so sure that she wanted to survive it either.

It was a full six weeks before Mary could be moved from her Italian hospital room, and then only with an incredible amount of pain. The special Med-Evac hospital flight back to the States was a nightmare, what she could remember of it. For the next eighteen months Mary recovered from the awful damage of the accident she should never have lived through.

Of course *recover* is a relative word. Physically, much like Jacob, Mary would always bear the marks of what happened. Emotionally she would never be the same person who so easily switched from one lifestyle to another. And spiritually, well, let's just say God got her attention.

Mary had a lot of time to think about her Lord and her faith, and what went wrong. I'm tempted to place her conversion here, but Mary's not so easily convinced that the faith of her youth was not a saving faith. I guess she's just a better covenantal theologian than I.

However one explains Mary's past, at long last her present was given over to the lordship of Jesus Christ. It was a personal commitment she was determined to keep with all the tenacity of soul that is born of suffering and surviving. Mary could no longer be moderate in her love for God.

I met Mary for the first time in my office with a young man we'll call Tim. They had been attending the church regularly because they were eager to learn the Scripture and quite serious about doing the will of God.

Tim had met Mary during her long convalescence. Both were very serious about their walk with God and both felt they were very much in love with each other. Nevertheless— and Mary was quite firm about this—marriage was out of the question unless she could be certain that it was within the will of God according to his Word.

They were coming to the church for help and clarity. Tim wanted to know if the elders of our church would prayerfully consider their situation and give them advice. The process took some time. Mary's former husband, who was not a believer, had since remarried and had a child. For Mary to return to her former husband was impossible. After prayer and deliberation, it was determined that for Mary and Tim marriage was not a violation of God's Word.

I had the privilege of sharing with both of them the decision of the elders in the matter. And I must admit, it was an emotional experience for me. I'm not sure that Mary and Tim understood what was so moving to me about the situation. Here was a couple, very much in love, in their late twenties, free to do whatever they chose to do (or so our society would have us believe). Nonetheless, they were willing to submit their hopes for personal happiness to the will of God.

It was a rare sight in my experience—two people not defiantly asking, "Why can't we get married?" but humbly saying, "We want to know whether our getting married is in the will of God." I knew without doubt that they were ready to accept whatever God's Word decreed, even if the answer were no.

But the answer was yes.

Mary and Tim were married in our church. And after several years, they remain a testimony to the grace of God and the healing power of his Word when it is obeyed by his people.

To my way of thinking, Mary and Tim's experience perfectly illustrates the fact that the complex decisions of life in moral arenas are not intended by God to be dealt with alone. The church is a place where help, counsel and clarity can be given with authority.

No, I am not trying to set up some kind of papal state among healthy Protestants. There is no pretension here to ecclesiastical infallibility. But I do believe that God blesses the process, however imperfect, of believers ministering to believers in critical moral areas. Such awesome responsibilities should be shared.

The buck stops with the local church, and it's high time the local church stopped passing the buck to the individual. Somehow, in such matters, the local church must learn to walk the straight and biblical line between authoritarian presumption and moral anarchy. The truth falls between two common human errors: the unethical takeover of individual responsibility by a group and the sad phenomenon of "every person doing right in his own eyes."

Both extremes must be avoided for the pitfalls that they are. But in spite of the cults and kooks who dominate a few unstable minds, our Protestant, evangelical world of the "rugged individual" needs to rediscover the corporate authority of the local church. This is particularly true in attempting to solve the moral complexities that surround the contemporary issues of divorce and remarriage.

The Irreplaceable Role of the Local Church

In the final analysis, the moral demands of complex life situations such as the role of the divorced and the remarried in the church can only be properly resolved by the Spirit of God. The Scripture teaches, however, that the Spirit will be operative among God's people, the church, only within the moral parameters of biblical truth. Going further, such truth must be applied discerningly, carefully and justly in the hands of the local church if the desired spiritual resolution of such serious complex situations is ever to be realized.

It should be abundantly clear from our Lord's rebukes of Pharisaism, as well as his teaching on the role of the church in solving human conflict in Matthew 18, that God is not only concerned about the moral *ends* of our lives but the *means* as well. The decisions we come to, as well as the ways we come to them, are equally important when dealing with matters of acute moral complexity.

The local church is God's agent in resolving serious matters of moral complexity. But from time to time, Christians seem to prefer the end-run approach. Forgive an old football term, but an end run figuratively means skirting the issues and running around problems rather than solving them in a straightforward and proper way. In this case, an end-run approach would take place when believers dash off seeking any and all alternatives to the local church in order to resolve their marital conflicts and concerns.

In 1 Corinthians 6 the apostle Paul clearly forbids Christians from taking this kind of approach in the case of possible wrongs and fraudulent treatment. The Corinthian Christians were making "end runs" by taking other believers into secular courts and bypassing the divinely appointed agent of reconciliation and justice among believers—the local church.

> When one of you has a grievance against a brother, does he dare go to law before the unrighteous instead of the saints? Do you not know that the saints will judge the world? And if the world is to be judged by you, are you incompetent to try trivial cases? (1 Cor 6:1-2)

This passage is not simply a negative prohibition forbidding Christians to litigate against other Christians. The real point is a positive one. It is that the church should be looked to in resolving conflicts among professing Christians. Sadly, at Corinth at least, the church had evidently resigned from its biblically mandated task, and individual believers were not turning to the church in hopes of reconciliation.

Christians were avoiding the church, and the church was avoiding a job it was supposed to do. Individual believers lacked respect for the church—evident in their refusal to come to the church for counsel and arbitration. In addition, the church lacked the nerve to attempt to bring justice to individual believers. This had apparently begun a devaluating spiral that was literally removing Christians from godly counsel and godly counselors from the church.

> If then you have such cases, why do you lay them before those who are least esteemed by the church? I say this to your shame. Can it be that there is no man among you wise enough to decide between members of the brotherhood? (1 Cor 6:4-5)

As some have aptly said in the field of physical therapy, "Use it or lose it." In Corinth the church was also suffering from a kind of atrophy—an atrophy of judgment. Individual Christians were driven to unacceptable extremes such as taking fellow believers to secular magistrates.

Are not Christians today doing much the same thing when they ignore their local assemblies and seek arbitration and reconciliation agencies outside the church? Does it make such "end runs" acceptable if these agencies are Christian? What about the erosion of respect concerning the church (that sets in subtly but assuredly) whenever believers "end run" the authority and obligations of the local church? Consequently, our lack of expectations for the church continues to sap it of its leadership and its will to be the church that Jesus called it to be.

This is not to say that Christian reconciliation agencies and Christian counseling services do not have a place. They most certainly have a very valuable and useful place in the Christian community. It is, however, important that their place be under the authority of a local church in matters touching the lives of those who are part of that local church.

Counseling programs and reconciliation services have a serious biblical obligation to make sure that their ministry is in harmony with and respectful of the authority of that local church which is over the lives of whomever seeks out their assistance. It should never be forgotten that it is the unmistakable conviction of Matthew 18 and other passages that the church itself is to be an agent of reconciliation.

The church and individuals in the church can certainly employ outside expertise in dealing with the complex problems of human conflict. But such steps should not be seen as the church relinquishing its authority. In the final analysis, such consultations could best be viewed as bringing as many resources as possible back to the church for a final evaluation and decision.

It is counterproductive when Christians "end run" the church, since the resolution of moral problems seems to be a major reason for the continuing existence of a local assembly in God's design for things.

The role of divorced and remarried people in the church

is a matter for the local church to decide. Such determinations should come from careful and prayerful deliberation on the part of godly leaders with regard to the specific facts of each individual situation. The role of divorced and remarried people in the local church should not be determined by an inflexible, unwritten general law of common consent. Human conflict is too complex for that sort of thing. Too easily such common consent moves the church to the lowest common denominator of its least mature members and not to the heights of the loftiest judgments of its most spiritual leaders.

The position of divorced and remarried people in the church should be viewed as a matter for sensitive examination within the protective confines and personal, caring context of a local church. The leadership of that church should respect the dignity and worth of these people as it applies the Word of God in a loving, redemptive and restorative way.

As the local assembly approaches the question of moral decisions, there are certain dead ends to avoid. In the next chapter we will consider some of the obstacles in our way as we seek to make right decisions.

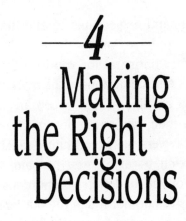

4
Making the Right Decisions

While [Jesus] was speaking, a Pharisee asked him to dine with him; so he went in and sat at table. The Pharisee was astonished to see that he did not first wash before dinner. And the Lord said to him, "Now you Pharisees cleanse the outside of the cup and of the dish, but inside you are full of extortion and wickedness. You fools! Did not he who made the outside make the inside also? But give for alms those things which are within; and behold, everything is clean for you.

"But woe to you Pharisees! for you tithe mint and rue

and every herb, and neglect justice and the love of God; these you ought to have done, without neglecting the others. Woe to you Pharisees! for you love the best seat in the synagogues and salutations in the market places. Woe to you! for you are like graves which are not seen, and men walk over them without knowing it."

One of the lawyers answered him, "Teacher, in saying this you reproach us also." And he said, "Woe to you lawyers also! For you load men with burdens hard to bear, and you yourselves do not touch the burdens with one of your fingers. Woe to you! for you build the tombs of the prophets whom your fathers killed. So you are witnesses and consent to the deeds of your fathers; for they killed them, and you build their tombs. Therefore also the Wisdom of God said, 'I will send them prophets and apostles, some of whom they will kill and persecute,' that the blood of all the prophets, shed from the foundation of the world, may be required of this generation, from the blood of Abel to the blood of Zechariah, who perished between the altar and the sanctuary. Yes, I tell you, it shall be required of this generation. Woe to you lawyers! for you have taken away the key of knowledge; you did not enter yourselves and you hindered those who were entering." (Lk 11:37-52)

Avoiding Externalism

In Luke 11, Jesus strikes at the very heart of Pharisaism. The Pharisees, we are told, were concerned only with externals, "the outside of the cup." With these concerns only, they neglected, in Matthew's words, "the weightier matters of the law" (Mt 23:23). Luke outlines these weightier matters as

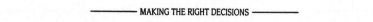

being justice and the love of God.

True, the ceremonial concerns of the Pharisees had a certain value. But these things, Jesus said, ought to be done without neglecting the greater issues of justice and mercy. A closer examination of Jesus' fierce rebuke of the Pharisees and scribes in Luke 11 will reveal that it was not prompted by their pompous hypocrisy, though that was bad enough. The anger of Jesus was kindled primarily because the legalistic charades of these institutionally pious frauds were destroying the lives of innocent people. Their concerns for mindless adherence to traditions and their unhealthy preoccupation with the appearances of things were defiling people (Lk 11:44); they were burdening people with impossible obligations and duties (Lk 11:46). Their hypocritical concerns were murderous (Lk 11:49), and the end result of their religious brutality was a complete obscuring of the Word of God from the experience of the common person (Lk 11:52).

When the followers of Jesus think of the roles of the divorced and remarried in the church, we had better be certain that our concerns are not simply the scribal concerns of the Pharisees for external appearances and punctilious observances of the supposed letter of the law. We had better take great care to demonstrate in all our ethical judgments the weightier matters of the law—justice and mercy.

Avoiding Judgmentalism

The guilt of the Pharisee and scribe went beyond simple hypocrisy. Jesus indicted them with the charge of sublime insensitivity regarding the crushing harshness of their teachings. Their opinions were crushing the life out of the innocent and eager hearts of sincere people.

The opinions we often so glibly speak and the manner in which we conduct our churches are very serious matters, particularly in regard to the question of divorced people. The questions concerning divorced people in the church are not merely matters of detached doctrinal interest; they will have lasting impact on the lives of men and women. Our opinions in some matters of doctrine, however ill-founded, poorly maintained and irrationally argued, are of little significance in the practical, day-to-day issues of life. But our convictions about divorce and remarriage may have serious repercussions in many people's lives.

We would do well to consider just how firmly our convictions are established according to the Scripture and how carefully they are presented in life, especially when considering the wounded and suffering.

Larry: The Man Who Listened Carefully

Several years back, when he was a very young Christian, Larry (as we will call him) was voted a place on a nominating committee in his local church. He eagerly pursued his responsibilities as a labor to the Lord. Larry was happy to finally have a real place of service in his church. He was, after all, a fairly new Christian. He had found the Lord in his early thirties. The circumstances surrounding his conversion involved a very painful divorce and separation from his children.

Larry had worked hard for his family—too hard. He was rarely home. His wife took solace in another man. In fact, in several other men. The marriage ended bitterly, but in the crisis Larry had made a serious and life-changing commitment to Christ. He was a new creation, and his new life was important to him.

One evening, as Larry met with the nominating committee, the question of qualification for church office arose. Larry listened stoically as another member of the nominating committee, a man Larry respected for his serious commitment to the Christian life, made an observation which Larry never forgot.

"We certainly cannot have people in leadership in the church who have ever had a divorce," the man Larry respected said. "After all, if they have been unfaithful once, they are liable to be unfaithful again."

The logic of that observation, not to mention its biblical support, was shaky to say the least. In the most charitable assessment, it was far too general, far too sweeping, far too inflexible. In short, it was far too unbiblical.

But Larry didn't know this. So he accepted it. As is often the case in the lives of new Christians, the Holy Spirit plants a very tender and submissive spirit there. Larry listened. Larry went home. And, without a great deal of noise, the very next day Larry resigned from his first position in the church. He quietly walked away from that which he wanted to do but was convinced he was ineligible to do. What was even sadder was that Larry carried the doubt of that blanket indictment into his Christian life for another ten years.

What we say in the church is often listened to, even when we may not be listening too carefully to what we say.

I think the point is clear enough. I don't know the man who said the things that Larry heard. I don't know his motives, but I am willing to say they were probably of the highest caliber. I am even willing to believe that the man never intended for Larry to draw the conclusions he did from such short, simple and general remarks. I would probably be safe in assuming that the man may have been willing to have Larry in leadership since his divorce and conversion were so close together. Many Christians have an easier time with preconversion divorce.

The fact is, however, that we will never know. The words were spoken with too little clarification and, as hindsight demonstrates, too little sensitivity. The man who said those things might have been saddened by Larry's overly harsh application of them to his own life. But the chances are he was never even aware of the impact of his hastily expressed opinions on the life of a young and troubled believer.

Why do we feel it necessary to often make the most difficult pronouncements in the strongest terms? Perhaps it is because our theological agendas often carry in our minds the same kind of notations that appeared on the sermon notes of a particular preacher which read: "Point is weak—holler!"

We often speak most judgmentally and absolutely when we are the least sure of ourselves. Our every idle word will be judged because, as is often the case, our idle words have lasting impact on the lives of those around us.

We will consider the issue of church leadership and divorce and remarriage later. In a real sense, before addressing the facts of that argument, a more important question faces us: How are we to share whatever truth we hold? As the Westminster divines said repeatedly in their catechisms, a

major proof of our doctrines' correctness lies in the impact it has on the lives of those who receive them. Do we speak our truth in love, or are there darker, less noble motivations behind our rush to judgment?

There is an interesting postscript to Larry's story. As I sat rereading it, almost a year after I first wrote it down, I decided to give Larry a call and let him know that the book was ready to be published. He seemed pleased. In our conversation Larry told me that he and his wife had recently applied for mission work with a board they had been supporting for several years. Larry was informed that, not only did the board *not* accept divorced people for mission work (even a preconversion divorce!), but they would not even allow their maintenance men to have ever been divorced! The mission representative seemed apologetic but, after all, he said, it was their policy. I wonder if "policy" falls inside or outside the cup.

Re-examining Our Restrictions

So often the discussion regarding divorced people in the church moves quickly to the negative. It is easy for such a discussion to become a discourse on what is or is not allowed by Scripture. A negative approach to ethics is an easy pitfall for conservative-minded people. And serious-minded Christians who hold to a strong view of Scripture and take sin seriously are conservative-minded in moral matters. And rightly so! As a result we often find the questions of prohibitions and restrictions rising in discussions about moral problems. Our concern is not "what can we get away with" but rather "what the Word of God allows."

However, in the light of Jesus' stinging rebuke of the more conservative members of his community (the Pharisees) who found it quite easy to lay all manner of restrictions on people, we should ask ourselves, "If restrictions and prohibitions must be placed on certain people because of unalterable and lasting circumstances, what is the purpose of our restrictions? What is gained by our prohibitions? What is the end result of our restrictions in terms of the outcome of their lives?" And, most important, "Where is justice and mercy in our application of God's Word?"

If our only answer is that our restrictions and prohibitions are intended to be an outward demonstration of holy standards, a statement of principle cast, as it were, in the lives of certain people through lifelong limitations of their Christian service, then one is tempted to wonder where justice and mercy fit in. Do not restrictions such as these come much too close to being merely hypocritical concerns for "the outside of the cup"? Do they not border on censorious and punitive acts of judgmentalism? It is not enough to follow the unquestioned practice of restrictions in the Christian community under the banner of a blind obedience to alleged biblical standards. Blind obedience, even to God's standards, is pharisaical and wrong.

On the other hand, if we are seeking by our community standards, by what we allow and what we do not allow, to make a statement concerning the grace of God and the forgiveness of Christ, should not a Christian church's response to the darkest of sinful situations be full and complete restorative forgiveness in the wake of fully confessed repentance? Unthinking restrictions which appeal to ceremonial holiness and cloud the gospel of grace are acts of Pharisaism.

Jim: The Man Who Missed His Wife

He came into my office in the early months of my pastoral career. Those were the "lamb-white days" of certainty for me. It was before life's complexities and a more intimate study of Scripture had softened my certainties.

For the sake of anonymity and the confidential aspects of pastoral counseling, I'll change his name to Jim, and alter just enough of the peripheral information to obscure his real identity.

Jim was in his fifties, quiet and unassuming, clearly committed to Christ. And he was lonely. Jim missed his wife and his son, now in his early twenties and still living with his mother. Several years back, after twenty years of marriage, Jim's wife became resolute. She did not want to be married and didn't want to see Jim again, ever.

With the considerable help of our state's streamlined divorce laws, her desire was quickly a fact. Jim was legally extracted from his home, most of his belongings, and from the side of his wife of twenty-five years and their son quicker than you could say "no fault."

Jim was a Christian. He did not oppose the action. And, in the words of Dick Van Dyke in a particularly unfunny comedy filmed in the sixties, "They split up the family gold mine. She got the gold and he got the shaft."

His wife was in another community, active in another church (which evidently didn't care too much about the situation) and leading another life, sans Jim. She got what she wanted and, for the first time that Jim could remember in a long time, seemed content.

Jim, however, was miserable. He came to my office for advice. As he sat with me he shared his story.

From almost the outset of his marriage, Jim knew something was wrong with his wife. For absolutely no reason that he could determine there would be days when she would glare at him and storm around the house in silent, tearful rage. Jim was a retail manager, and this fury would greet him in the morning as he left for work and be waiting for him in the evening when he returned from a long, hard day.

Finally, it burst open. "You're having an affair, aren't you?" She screamed it at him one morning as he was about to leave for work. He was dumbfounded. His wife told him that she knew that he was committing adultery with one of his female employees. "You've betrayed me, and I hate you."

Jim was devastated. There was only one thing wrong with what his wife was accusing him of. Jim was then and remained ever-faithful to his wife. No, he was not "seeing" someone else. No, he was not unfaithful to his wife.

The one thing wrong with what Jim was saying was that his wife wouldn't believe him. Try as he would to convince her, she remained adamant.

"You're being unfaithful to me."

No amount of assurance to the contrary could sway her convictions. After the next few days it became obvious that she was voicing her convictions to their friends in the church. As is so often the case, her reports of Jim's infidelity were received by her friends. They were a sympathetic and somewhat eager audience. But nothing was done.

"Let's pray about it. Maybe it (or he?) will go away," seemed to be the prevailing attitude. Finally, in desperation, as much to convince his wife as to overcome his shame, Jim offered to quit his promising job and move to another state. He would never see this girl (whoever she was) again.

This decision seemed to mollify his wife. They left town quickly. Sadly, soon after in another city, in another state, in another church and with another job, Jim's wife began a repeat performance.

Several years, many moves and one child later, Jim began to suspect mental illness. It was not something a Christian likes readily to admit. He pleaded with her to see a doctor. She resolutely refused. The thought of psychological help repulsed her and drove her into deeper rage.

"They're all unbelievers," she argued. "They would think your disgusting behavior with other women would be just fine." The case was closed. And so, it seemed to Jim, was his life.

I can't tell you why Jim never sought help himself. I think he was too ashamed. Everyone knows that Christians aren't supposed to have problems, right?

I can't tell you why Jim didn't appeal to the church to have his problems resolved. I can only observe the sad fact that I never even asked him the question. At that period of my life, even as a pastor, the idea that anyone would seek out the church for an authoritative role in solving problems between people was as unfamiliar to me as it was to Jim.

I'm not sure what Bible I wasn't reading then, but Jim wasn't reading the same one. Jim's private hell lasted over twenty years. Hysterical charges, tearful denials, shame, gossip, more moves and more new jobs. Finally it became intolerable. Not for Jim, but for his wife. The divorce came and Jim went into a deep depression.

He came to me. His rented room was collapsing in on itself like some kind of tacky black hole that he was in the middle of. His work was boring; his life felt barren. What could he do? His loneliness screamed to him night after sleepless night.

Jim had attended conservative Bible churches most of his adult life. He was certain that divorce was a great sin in his life. He felt sure that remarriage, under any circumstances, was unthinkable. He actually had no prospects, and he cursed himself for even imagining in moments of weakness that he could ever share his life with a sane and happy woman. So he came to me for advice.

How do you make someone comfortable in hell? I listened in silence. Then, with all the sober wisdom that a twenty-seven-year-old could muster (like the medieval scholar of whom it was said, "he was often in error, but never in doubt"), I spoke with absolute conviction:

"All divorce is sin," I said comfortingly. "And for you, of course, remarriage is out of the question," I said to give him hope. "Maybe reconciliation is possible," I finished lamely.

He just looked up at me. We were both sitting down, but his head was hanging much lower than mine. His hands were folded lifelessly between his knees. He looked like a man trying, but just too tired to pray. All at once I felt as if I were walking him down some long, last corridor toward the electric chair—only I wasn't the chaplain, I was the executioner.

I made a final effort to say something positive. "Jim, why don't you let the church be your family? Let her be your wife!" I had placed my hand on his shoulder. He didn't recoil when I said that, he just sort of . . . shrunk.

I sat there, a twenty-seven-year-old clergyman, and watched a fifty-year-old, lonely little man dissolve into a reservoir of twenty-year-old tears. It wasn't silent weeping. They were deep, heart-rending sobs.

After a time he quietly rose to go. He thanked me as he shook my hand. There was no irony or bitterness in him.

Shortly after that, Jim found a better job in a community about fifty miles to the south. I ran into him several years later in a shopping mall. He looked ten years younger and almost radiant.

With little comment, but a great deal of kindness, he greeted me and told me that about a year ago he had married a fine Christian woman and they were working together in a local church serving the Lord and were very much in love.

Until the day I die, I will thank God that Jim didn't take my advice.

Something was terribly wrong in my response to Jim's need, and I should have known it. That was my problem—I was suffering from "systems failure," which is fancy, high-tech jargon for "a fly in the ointment." And the buzzing of those flies in my ointment was deafening. Sometimes I'm a slow study, but I caught on. I finally put my finger on my systemic flaw.

You've probably seen the routine in a hundred comedies and cartoons. The dumb cluck (be it Stanley or Oliver; Mickey or Goofy) decides to save money and build the house himself. When he's done it's lovely, a picture of domestic beauty. The only trouble is when they go to take a bath and turn on the hot water, the radio plays out of the spigot. Worse than that, when anyone rings the doorbell, they get a shower.

It may be funny in a comedy, but it can be tragic in a church. Such unexpected results are sure signs of systemic flaws. When you turn on the kitchen light, you are not supposed to get ice cubes. When water runs out of your bedside reading lamp, you had best check the plumbing. Your plumbing system is supposed to give water, and your electrical system is supposed to give light.

Would that we were as analytical with our doctrine! God's truth is supposed to produce love and peace. ("The aim of our charge," Paul said of his biblical instruction to Timothy, "is love that issues from a pure heart"—1 Tim 1:5.) God's truth cleanses and restores in hope and holiness. ("You were washed, you were sanctified"—1 Cor 6:11.)

When the results of our "system" are shame and alienation, hopelessness and despair, my friend, we are suffering from systems failure. Look closely at your system. God's Word is consistent, each part enhancing the whole with the glory of God, each part never contradicting its gracious sum. There must be a harmonious consistency to all of God's truth.

Now look closely at your view of divorce and remarriage in the church. Has it become the only sin with lasting effects in spite of God's grace? Has divorce become that unique exception in your thinking which makes it unlike any other sin?

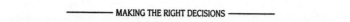

There is a grotesque and ludicrous exaggeration that somehow still makes a telling point. I was once told in jest that if my wife were unfaithful to me, I should kill her, because the church forgives murderers and allows them ministry, but never the divorced. As ridiculous as it is, this is too uncomfortably close to the truth! It ably demonstrates that there is a flaw in many doctrinal systems.

A great deal is at stake here. When the ill-fated space shuttle Challenger exploded before the eyes of a horrified nation seventy-four seconds into its final mission, the cold and lifeless voice of ground control was heard to say, "There appears to have been a major malfunction." "Malfunction," or as the engineers would later refer to as "systems failure," is perhaps too clinical a term for our use, however accurate.

The fact is that people get hurt when there are systemic flaws and systems failures, whether they are flaws in the booster rocket of a space craft or in the doctrine that governs the lives of people in the church.

Going God One Better
The Pharisees were guilty of a legalism that brutalized people. Their inflexibility of principle obscured the mercy and love of God. This was often done by a principle of "going God one better." The process is simple. One moves from the heart of what God allows to the boundaries of what is prohibited. Then, stepping back into the permissible, one draws new lines of prohibition defined by the self, not the Lord.

If God said, "Do not eat of the fruit," Eve would loudly proclaim, "Neither should you touch it." If God said, "Do no

work on the Sabbath," the Pharisee would say, "Do not heal withered hands either." To this mentality, bettering God is a safe approach to questions of obedience and faith. Hyper-legalism and simplistic reductions of complex situations into the monosyllabic formula No seem safer to some than the more difficult demands of balanced judgment and the reasonable use of Scripture.

Jesus' disciples almost "went God one better" in response to the Lord's teaching on divorce. In Matthew 19, after Jesus makes it very clear that divorce is a serious matter and not at all as trivial as the lawyers and rabbis had tried to make it, his disciples respond in the typical mode. The disciples said to him, "If such is the case of a man with his wife, it is not expedient to marry" (Mt 19:10).

Fortunately the Lord has never accepted the brutal purity of total denial or of "going God one better" in the face of moral complexity.

> But he said to them, "Not all men can receive this saying, but only those to whom it is given. . . . He who is able to receive this, let him receive it." (Mt 19:11-12)

Jesus cared about the needs of people, and he quickly rejected the all-too-human tendency to adopt an inhuman legalism. As the progress of truth within the church would illustrate, people carried this habit of bettering God to its ultimate end—heresy.

> Now the Spirit expressly says that in later times some will depart from the faith by giving heed to deceitful spirits and doctrines of demons, through the pretensions of liars whose consciences are seared, who forbid marriage and enjoin abstinence from foods which God created to be

received with thanksgiving by those who believe and know the truth. (1 Tim 4:1-3)

Augustine was referring to the process of bettering God when he said, "Most men prefer total abstinence to perfect moderation." In other words, many people prefer the simple motto: "When in doubt, throw it out." This may be a good dictum when you are sorting through damaged fruit or looking for rotten eggs, but when you are dealing with human lives, something a bit more sensitive and delicate is required.

Is this the process behind the thinking that says since the Bible forbids divorce as sin, anyone who so sins is to be forever relegated to a secondary position in the fellowship? This sort of nonsequacious reasoning is surely the product of "going God one better."

Avoiding Relativism

The dangers of bettering God are clear. An escalating insensitivity to human need inevitably follows. Nevertheless, there is a danger on the other end of the spectrum as well. In a modern world that despises moral absolutes and questions biblical authority, there is a definite danger of relativism. Discarding all principle, even on the pretext of being compassionate, can often be a cynical smoke screen employed by those who in reality have no respect or love for the biblical principles that are precious to the orthodox believer.

The proper response, however, is not a siege mentality. Our response should not be a call for making our standards even higher. On the contrary, it is a time for discernment on a greater scale than perhaps has ever yet been called for. Ours is a time for the local church to come together as Jesus

prescribed in Matthew 18. Without fear, the church must enter into judgment, comforted in the realization that "where two or three are gathered," Jesus is present with them. This being so, the things that are bound on earth as well as the things that are loosed on earth will most certainly reflect the opinions of heaven.

Divorce and remarriage are matters for the local church to deal with under the rule of Scripture and guidance of the Spirit of Christ. Each case must be dealt with separately and with great care. The roles of Christian service following such an upheaval as divorce must also be decided upon by the local church. In their decisions, remarriage also should be dealt with from a critical and analytical perspective.

The Fine Art of Despising the Church

There is a subtle and altogether delightful phrase afoot in the English-speaking world: "damned through faint praise." It says so much. The more refined and sophisticated a society becomes, the more a subtle concept such as this makes regular appearances.

Honest repudiation and open expressions of dislike make people increasingly uncomfortable in well-mannered, if not overly mannered, society. The brazen insult, the hostile declamation are seen today as indications of the speaker's uncouth and ill-mannered nature. In other words, to insult too openly is simply uncivilized.

More than that, in our ever more psychologized world, an open and unmistakenly expressed dislike is said to reveal our own "hang-ups" rather than expose a problem somewhere else. People who utter negatives too quickly or injudiciously are likely to be labeled "defensive"—and God forbid that anyone be forced to bear that ultimate malediction in today's genteel society. If one should ever be labeled defensive, one runs the risk of being dismissed for having "unresolved tensions" rather than legitimate grievances.

With the laissez-faire mores of the '80s, is there such a thing as a legitimate grievance anyway?

Poor critic! If we are too open with our disapproval, we may quickly find ourselves bearing the worst of all Cain's marks. In the land of the laid back, anyone indignant is soon dismissed as "too uptight." Such a sin is not to be mentioned, even among the Gentiles.

To be a modern critic one needs a refined sense of subtlety. If the critic is to escape criticism, he or she must master the literary equivalents of the art of sleight of hand: the verbal feint, the double entendre, the ability to "damn through faint praise."

With such refined expressions, the level of cruelty rises in almost direct proportion to the restraint of language. And faint praise can be devastating. If a book review labels a 600-page history of the Reformation which took its author twenty years to compile, as "competent" and "one of a number of adequate surveys of the period," chances are it will collect more dust than royalties for its author.

If a motion picture is described as a "modest first effort, which is at times witty," the vast moviegoing public, looking for the laugh hit of the decade, will stay away from this "modest" and "witty" film in droves.

If a scholarship committee, looking for outstanding academic achievement, informs you in an interview that you are a "solid and conscientious student," you would be well advised to consider other tuition options immediately.

When a major university scout describes Jones as a "solid, scrappy little guy for a lineman, and his lack of speed is compensated by his positive mental outlook," it's time for Jones to consider the joys of the smaller college.

"Scrappy" is no substitute for "gargantuan"; "solid" is not the same as "brilliant" and "positive mental outlooks" dissolve under the scrutiny of the major college recruiter who is looking for the "agile, mobile and hostile" superstar of the major college productions.

As for the modest, witty little film, the hoi polloi want belly laughs, not wit; and anyone willing to suffer through six-hundred pages of Reformation history wants this generation's best, not something merely competent.

The modern critic with an axe to grind knows this. And through the judicious use of faint praise he or she is able to place that axe directly between the shoulder blades without leaving so much as a fingerprint.

Damning through faint praise, the operational insult of the terminally polite, suits our refined culture admirably.

Obliging the Devil

The strange contradictions of our overly nice society were observed long ago by William Buckley in his book *Up From Liberalism*. Buckley speaks of our terminally polite society as "the obliging generation" who would say things like, "Mr. Hitler is no gentleman," but would happily shake the bloody hand of Chou En Lai at an embassy cocktail party. We are people who shake hands but never come out fighting.

Edmond Rostand gave Cyrano a line that was intended to indict the overcivilized hypocrisy of sixteenth-century French morals. Sick to death of sycophants, flatterers and the insincere manners of the literati, Cyrano in his integrity longed for an honest foe amid his mob of so-called friends.

"Just once," he tells La Brett, "let me be able to look up and say, 'here, thank God, comes an enemy.' "

But how can Christians *love* their enemies today? They refuse even to recognize them. Like Cyrano, it's high time to start thanking God if at long last we can say, "That is evil," or "Here comes an enemy."

Sadly, Christians all too easily succumb to the dictates of an obliging generation. We seldom say much bad about anything or anybody. And quite unlike Cyrano, we never admit the existence of an enemy, let alone look for one.

Oh, you still might hear some fading, strident echoes in the fire-and-brimstone preaching of a few—usually on 1500-watt radio stations in certain rural counties of Georgia and Mississippi. But it's all a vast retreating roar these days.

It seems we're far more concerned with feeling good than with feeling bad. And who can fault that? But there is little room for a Jeremiah in our happy age.

Simmer, Don't Boil

To detect evangelical moral indignation, one must learn to read between the sentimental lines of Christian journalism. Unfortunately one must look quickly. Moral outrage rarely survives the restraint of our mores and manners or the niceties of the dispassionate, if well-turned, phrase.

Still, human nature does have its murky side, even when

throttled by convention. And all of us, in every age (with apologies to Mr. Poe), "draw our passions from a common spring." In short, we seethe.

Our "negative vibes" reverberate, however discreetly, across the strings of faint praise. Hostility, in many evangelical circles, appears in the tacit understanding: "If you can't say something good about someone or something, then . . . say something a little less good."

We must admit the truth, even at the risk of walking lockstep with our overpsychologizing Weltgeist, that our faint praise often betrays certain unconscious attitudes that are decidedly negative.

Minority advocates have often done battle with such phenomena. For example, certain clichés drive astute feminists to the barricades. Pepper any conversation with Gloria Steinem with observations concerning, for example, "the good little woman" you married or the "great little gal" who is your secretary, and watch the fun. Tell Andrew Young that he's a "fine boy," and you'll see the flames from as far away as Plains.

"She's pretty smart, for a woman" or "He's a reliable black man" carry entire hidden agendas of prejudice and contempt. One wonders now why former President Eisenhower ever dared claim he was a "conservative with a heart." (A right-wing acquaintance of mine responded to that by saying he was a liberal with a brain. Can we survive such civility long?)

The tones of faint praise quite often meld with the unconscious expressions of disdain in the evangelical-speak of the pulpit, magazine and paperback book.

On Target

The most abused victim of faint praise among the saints militant is the local church. Certainly no one dare speak against the concept of the church openly—after all, it is biblical. But to be sure, we can all be critics of the church, questioning its function and its structure. This is usually a healthy activity. But far greater damage is done to the church by the polite paternalism of many Christians than by either the fiercest enemies or her most unkind critic.

I have, for instance, promised myself the blessed oblivion of madness if one more elderly lady speaks cloyingly to me of "her little church." (God forbid, I have even heard references to "my little pastor." I think I'm becoming a little ill.)

Some Christians—with the benign neglect of diminished respect, with low esteem ringing from every syllable of faint praise—are doing greater damage to the church than hell ever could.

At the risk of appearing paranoid, I will amplify what is meant by some common faint praise regarding the local church.

It's a good little church . . . *as far as churches go.*

He's a fine pastor. . . . *Of course he's no Bible college president.*

The church is a high calling. . . . *If you're lucky, in five years or so you'll be able to teach at a seminary or do something really important.*

Church attendance is important. . . . *But if you really want to meet God, or be ministered to, you ought to attend this conference or hear this special speaker.*

Is there any doubt that the church today is being paternalized, reduced, tolerated and damned by faint praise?

Zero Expectations

To many, church is increasingly seen as something which Christians know they must be a part of but really don't want to be. The church is too often endured but not endearing.

The old story about the door-to-door vacuum salesman relates to this. His sales were nonexistent. Finally, his supervisor went with him as he visited potential customers. After his first sentence it was obvious what the problem was.

Worn and bedraggled, with a hangdog expression across his careworn countenance, his listless finger probed for the doorbell. When the door opened he spoke his opening line:

"You don't wanta buy a vacuum, do ya?"

Somehow, this story captures the, shall we say, lack of enthusiasm that surrounds many people's concept of church.

I suppose a brief disclaimer is in order before I begin to beat the drum for a change in the American evangelical's benign contempt for the local church. I hold the conviction that the local church is being treated with contempt by Christians today, although I myself have had a wonderful personal experience as a pastor for over fifteen years. I say this not to sound my own horn, but to keep my observations from being dismissed as merely the dismal, sour-grape grumblings of a disgruntled ministerial misfit.

I have been privileged to experience some very productive years as a pastor. I have seen our church, in a highly transient university community, grow from 30 to 500 people. We have seen literally thousands pass through our doors for relatively short stays.

My pulpit ministry has been well received and, through thick and thin, the vast majority of those with whom I have ministered have been supportive and loving to the extreme. We have seen nearly seventy young men and women give their lives to full-time Christian service. We have even survived a major building program together. I do not view these things as my personal achievements, but they have been my positive experiences.

Our church has seen an exciting life together in the Lord. Perhaps because of this we have been able to plant six other churches in our part of the country. For all of this I am grateful to God.

Nevertheless, I am convinced that the local church is being abused, patronized and neglected in the modern evangelical world. And something must be done to reverse this almost unconscious contempt of the local church, this malaise of the mind that says in essence, "expect nothing of the local church and you won't be disappointed."

When I first began talking with people who might form the nucleus of new churches in strategic communities, I repeatedly encountered a similar situation. A group would come to me and share how their particular fellowship or Bible study in their home was so vital to them. They would say how they longed for more Bible teaching, fellowship, prayer and opportunities to share their faith in Christ.

I would join in their enthusiasm and say, "It sounds like you are becoming a church together."

"Oh no!" they would invariably reply, "We want Bible study, fellowship, prayer and opportunities to share our faith.

We don't want church!"

When did the local church begin to seem to many as the antithesis of vibrant life together in the Spirit? When did it become this thing endured but not endearing?

We need a fresh reminder of what the local church was intended to be. We need to see the local church as Scripture envisions it. It is not something to be tolerated in the world. It is, rather, to be something unleashed upon the world.

True, the local church must be more relevant, more vibrant, more alive—all the old clichés. But before any outward attempts to change the church can succeed, we must once again restore the biblical concept of the church in our own thinking.

We must be convinced again from Scripture of the local church's highest priority in our lives. We must renovate our esteem of the church before we overhaul the church itself.

It is imperative that the "expect nothing" mindset be replaced with the highest expectations for the local church.

American Christians are going to have to put the church among their highest priorities in life. This might be assisted by some strategic thinking. Jesus said where our treasure is, there our heart would be also (Mt 6:21). We would do well to consider just what it is in life that we treasure most.

It is a simple truth that the greatest treasure for many Americans is their profession. To others it is their houses. We move in and out of communities by the dictates of our job, the resale value of our house, or the proximity of good schools and parks. But to some people the most important factor in locating where they will live is the existence of a sound local church.

I have known believers who have turned down lucrative jobs in other parts of the country because they felt the ministry of a certain local church was more important in their lives and the lives of their families than the amount of money they could earn or the amount of power they could wield. On the other hand, there are certain Christians to whom there is no question as to where their loyalty lies. If the job beckons, off they go. If a bigger house is possible, then a bigger house it is. To what degree does the importance of our local church determine the true priorities of our life? If our commitment to a local church were costly enough, perhaps we would not settle for irrelevance and mediocrity in a local church.

If our inward expectations are reformed, we will do whatever is necessary to conform the outward reality of a local church to the biblical ideal. Of course the biblical ideal will never be realized. In this fallen world we must be "becomers," never feeling we have attained the ultimate. But if our respect and esteem of the local church is revitalized by God's Spirit, we will once again start to experience New Testament effectiveness in our lives.

If our esteem and respect for the idea of the local church is what it should be, Jesus' command to allow the church to have an effective role in the resolution of conflict will no longer be foreign or painful. It will become a creative option of hope.

Once the argument is won and the case for the local church's indisputable role in resolving moral conundrums like divorce is granted, where do you go? Obviously mechanisms need to be hammered out to assist the church in an orderly assessment of the situations it is called upon to adjudicate.

Policies such as the one I will outline below are needed to assist the local church as it wends its way through the treacherous mazes of human complexity. It is comforting to know Jesus' promise: "There am I in the midst of them" (Mt 18:20).

A Possible Mechanism for Making Decisions

"If you find a perfect church," Billy Graham is reported to have observed, "don't join it; you'll ruin it." The eternal truth behind this tongue-in-cheek dictum is that there is no such thing as a perfect church. It is equally true that, this side of paradise, there are no perfect plans for church action, particularly in the sensitive matter of divorce.

Nevertheless, plans of action are called for, and many of them. They should be drafted prayerfully under the searchlight of Scripture, and they should be fine-tuned in the demanding "road test of life."

In the issue of whether or not someone in the church is eligible for a divorce, it is critical for a sensitive mechanism to be drafted to guide church leaders toward a sound decision. I close this chapter with a simple guideline that has assisted one particular church in its wrestling with the questions. To some it may be helpful, to others it may seem inadequate. To those in the latter camp I can only reply, "Go thou and do better."

I want to preface what I say about decision-making procedures by emphasizing the role of church leadership in settling the difficult questions that surround divorce. The church structure that I am most familiar with and that best reflects my ecclesiastical convictions places a group of elders at the point of highest leadership in a local church. These people exercise broad discretionary authority under the approval and submissive willingness of the congregation in regards to the spiritual directions of the church and to the moral problems that might, from time to time, confront it. It is not necessary, however, to follow a single pattern of church government in order to respond to the Matthew 18 process in the ways that will be outlined. Nevertheless, whatever titles church leaders bear and whatever functions they perform, it seems undeniable from a scriptural perspective that church leadership, at the highest level, is a corporate matter. There should be a group of people guiding the church.[1]

In the hands-on aspects of church discipline and order, vis-à-vis the instructions of Matthew 18, a corporate approach to church discipline can best implement the process. This is why Galatians 6:1 advises:

Brethren, if a man is overtaken in any trespass, you [plural] who are spiritual should restore him in a spirit of gentleness. Look to yourself, lest you too be tempted.

Here, as in Matthew 18, the Scripture is clear that the objective of church discipline is the restoration of the offender. This was also the heart concern of Jesus: "If he listens to you, you have gained your brother" (Mt 18:15). But the matter of sin among Christians is a sensitive, complex and even dangerous thing. The possibilities of getting enmeshed in sin yourself while trying to extricate someone else from it are great. "Look to yourself," Paul warns, "lest you too be tempted." There is an abrupt change from the plural "you who are spiritual" to the singular "look to yourself." Bishop Lightfoot commented that this abrupt change "gives the charge a direct personal application."[2] Fredrick Rendall goes even further,

> The transition from the plural . . . to the singular . . . is instructive. The treatment of offenders belonged to the Church collectively, but each member needed to examine himself individually.[3]

From Galatians 6:1 we can conclude that issues of church discipline should be dealt with collectively and that individual involvement is fraught with potential risk. Involvement in church discipline requires the cooperative efforts of the most mature hearts and minds. Hopefully, the most mature hearts and minds of any church reside in the people who lead it.

Beyond this, there is the problem of confidentiality. The delicate matters of private, personal problems between Christians, if unresolved, must be brought to the church. But in saying this, it is certainly not intended that such private and personal matters be forced into a total public disclosure. In matters of personal concern, the will of the church should be directed by its highest leadership, whether these leaders are called elders, deacons, trustees or whatever. The privacy and dignity of individuals should be guarded by those who lead the church.

Making a group of church leaders representatives for the whole church in directing spiritual decisions certainly reflects much scriptural teaching. Just as the writer to the Hebrews directs his fellow believers who reside in local churches to "obey your leaders and submit to them; for they are keeping watch over your souls, as men who will have to give account" (Heb 13:17), so also the apostle Peter encourages the elders in local churches to "tend the flock of God that is your charge" (1 Pet 5:2).

In matters of the work of the church, Paul is very clear:

We beseech you, brethren, to respect those who labor among you and are over you in the Lord and admonish you, and to esteem them very highly in love because of their work. (1 Thess 5:12–13)

Whatever their titles, the leaders are responsible to be involved in the work of the church. Church discipline is certainly a major work. The leadership of the church can best follow the general directions of Matthew 18, and best accommodate those who are seeking to follow Jesus' clear instruction to "tell it to the church."

In telling it to the church, according to Matthew 18, one should bring the facts of the problem ultimately before the leadership of the church. In my thinking, this certainly involves the pastor-teacher, but reaches beyond any one authority. It reaches to the highest church authority, and the highest church authority best resides in a group of leaders who must render wise and serious judgments on behalf of the entire church. What follows then is a suggested procedure designed to help the church come to the wise and serious judgments that are needed by the people of God.

A Possible Procedure for Elder Involvement in Questions of Divorce

1. A credible report of the facts in the situation must be confirmed to the elders by two or three reliable witnesses.

2. The elders must decide whether the dissolution of the marriage is allowable within the biblical parameters. This decision is neither counsel for nor against divorce at this time. It is important to preserve the proper function of the

elders at this point. They are not acting as personal counselors, though they should certainly be ready to give counsel. At this point they are only attempting to establish proper moral guidelines, not only for the people in question, but for the benefit of the whole church.)

3. Having made this decision, the elders must meet with either or both parties.

4. This meeting may be accomplished by a select committee of three or four elders.

5. During this meeting:

a. It must be clearly communicated that the elder board as a general rule does not advise anyone to seek a divorce.

b. It must be clearly and compassionately communicated that God hates divorce.

c. It must be clearly communicated whether or not the elders see the evidence presented by the innocent party as acceptable grounds for divorce.

d. Finally, the elders must communicate a willingness to provide further spiritual, emotional and physical support through the entire crisis, praying for reconciliation if at all possible, and maintaining proper moral discipline in the situation.

A Lay Response

As this chapter on decision making draws to a close, we note that the bulk of the advice given here is directed to the leadership of the local church. But what of the average member of the congregation who, though not necessarily possessed of all the facts in a given situation, must still live with the emotional wreckage?

One inescapable word is this: divorce is a tragedy. The few times it has menaced our congregation it was like death; grief was heavy. Likewise, caring for and loving those who have gone through divorce and accepting those who are trying to put their Christian lives together again in the aftermath of divorce is demanding. How can we respond?

For a start, take heart! When you reach out to a needy brother or sister in love and open yourself up to him or her, you are doing what the Lord Jesus wants you to do.

Another very liberating realization is that you don't have to be a judge in every situation. As Paul reminds us in Romans 14, speaking, as he does, of a hypothetical Christian with a certain hypothetical problem, "before his own master he stands or falls" (v. 4). The very personal matters that must be considered in deciding on the propriety of divorce and remarriage should not be shared with every member of the congregation. Christians who are following the biblical counsel to "tell it to the church" should be protected and dealt with in a private and sensitive way by those in leadership in that church. This means that church leaders will have to give account of their decision to God as "they are keeping watch over your souls" (Heb 13:17). The regular church member does not always have to be ready to voice his or her sovereign opinion on every issue.

Certainly, the approach I advocate here of the church community who faces moral problems together is open to abuse. Of course church leaders are capable of making wrong decisions. And church members should not be encouraged to accept, uncritically, flagrant violations of biblical morality even if it is accepted by those who are leaders in the church. Nor is it ever intended that church leaders are to be seen as always unquestionably right in what they decide or decree.

Nevertheless, the Lord Jesus has promised to bless and providentially direct the affairs of his church when we wrestle with the moral difficulties of life. This is not a guarantee of infallibility in decisions, but it is a promise in which the local church must have hope. After all is said, faith and hope should characterize the church of Jesus Christ, particularly in the darker hours of difficult decision making.

Simply stated, congregations must learn to respect good leadership and also to respect the need for a certain degree of privacy in delicate decisions concerning the lives of vulnerable people. We should remember that if there are leaders "over [us] in the Lord" (1 Thess 5:12) and if we are pleased to be under their pastoral care in the assembly, then we must learn how to "submit to the elders" (1 Pet 5:5).

In the face of the inevitable temptation to gossip, determine to say only good things—words that are full of hope and encouragement. Nothing throws a wet blanket on gossip like good words.

In the face of discomfort and embarrassment, determine to be courageous. Be bold to extend your kindness to those who need your love in spite of the awkwardness it might involve.

In short, there are innumerable things that a congregation can do to support their leadership in restoring those who are considering or experiencing divorce. They can all be summed up in one four-letter word: L-O-V-E.

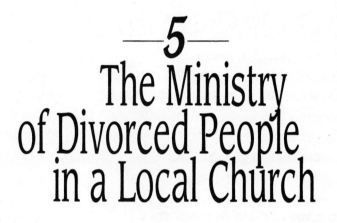

5

The Ministry
of Divorced People
in a Local Church

What is the role of the divorced and the remarried in Christian service? We can examine this question from the following analytical perspective.

First, there are two kinds of service within a local church. There is Christian ministry according to gifts of the Spirit which is demanded of every believer. A more specialized ministry involves functional positions of leadership that cannot be exercised by every believer constantly and must be engaged in only by those of the highest character.

Second, there are two kinds of situations for divorced people in the church. There are those who are divorced and have not remarried. And there are those who have divorced and subsequently remarried.

Third, there are two kinds of moral conditions pertaining to divorced people in the church—though usually no one is completely free of sin in such situations.[1] There is the situation where one party is essentially innocent while the other is essentially guilty. And there is the situation where both parties are essentially guilty.

The Issue of Guilt or Innocence

The question of guilt or innocence is important in any Christian's consideration of whether or not to seek divorce as well as whether or not to seek remarriage. This is clear from the "exception clause" in Matthew 5. As we have seen, in that passage Jesus allows for divorce in the wake of sexual sin. The potential sin of adultery by remarriage is ruled out when one of the marriage partners is guilty of sexual sin.

Paul also teaches about the question of guilt or innocence in 1 Corinthians 7 where, in the case of believers who are deserted by unbelievers, he declares that "God has called [his people] to peace" (v. 15). In such cases, Paul stated, the believer is not "bound" in marital obligation (1 Cor 7:15) and is therefore "freed" from a mate (1 Cor 7:27). Though Paul would prefer, as he always does, that remarriage not take place, he makes it clear that if there is a remarriage "you do not sin" (1 Cor 7:28). Paul concludes his teaching by making sure that we understand that those who are no longer bound in marriage (as in the case of death) have the freedom to remarry. But, Paul cautions, we should make sure the new mate is a believer. Paul commands that Christians marry "in the Lord" (1 Cor 7:39). (An examination of these two passages appeared in chapter two.)

However, the real problem comes when those who are admittedly guilty in the matter of a divorce choose, at a later time, to remarry. What is to be done if those, who break their marriage vows without just cause, earnestly seek God's forgiveness in repentance later in their lives?

Is divorce to be regarded by God's people as the one sin that is unlike any other sin? Is divorce to become the one sin for which there is only *conditional* forgiveness? Are we to teach that those in the past who were guilty of sins such as promiscuity, profligacy, perversion or even murder may find full release from their sin, but that the divorced cannot be granted full forgiveness and restoration in the church? If so, irreparable damage will be done to the perception of God's grace within the community of God's people—not to mention the insult done to his justice.

After cutting through all the complexities in situations of divorce and remarriage, we come to one basic fact. When a sinner expresses true repentance, and that true repentance is demonstrated by a consistent life of godliness, there is no biblical support for withholding him permanently from full participation in the life of the Christian community. And the emphasis in that last sentence should fall most heavily on the word *full.*

Any attempt by a church to withhold an honestly repentant Christian permanently from full participation in the life of the Christian community poses a grave threat not only to that church but to the Christian community in general. It devalues our understanding of God's grace and the nature of the atonement. It makes it difficult for all believers to comprehend, in the fullest sense, the redemptive work of Christ.

In those tragic times when divorce shatters a marriage, as well as in those confusing times when the prospects of remarriage are considered, it is imperative for God's people to come to judgment. And, in the process of judgment, all the matters of practical wisdom are secondary to the fundamental issue of whether or not God fully forgives and restores a sinner and whether or not God's people will fully forgive and receive a sinner. After establishing this fundamental issue, then the practical concerns of propriety should be considered. Both the individuals involved and the church as a whole should be patient and willing for a reasonable amount of time to elapse for healing and for good judgment to be arrived at and exercised. Undo haste in matters of divorce and remarriage can be destructive.

Church Discipline: Punishment or Restoration?

A fundamental fact of church discipline must be affirmed at this point. In the New Testament the only permanent results ever sought by God's people through the imposition of church discipline were complete repentance, reconciliation and restoration. In short, the church is not a penal institution. Though it is difficult to comprehend in a society where legitimate penal institutions have lost all thought of punishment in an alleged concern for rehabilitation, the church must not cave into the almost irresistible craving to exact due and just punishment.

In God's plan for society, the church was the original rehabilitation center. Scripture calls such rehabilitation redemption, reconciliation, regeneration and sanctification. The church is to be concerned with restoration. When restrictions arise from disciplinary responses within the church, all such restrictions imposed by church discipline are hoped to be temporary. They carry with them, as their primary concern, the sole intention of bringing every party to full repentance. We are not trying to create a group of second-class Christians.

Among the harshest passages on discipline in the New Testament are 1 Timothy 1:20 and 1 Corinthians 5:5. Nevertheless we can still observe that moral correction was the ultimate goal of both passages.

Hymenaeus and Alexander [were delivered to Satan *that they may learn not to blaspheme.* (1 Tim 1:20—emphasis mine)

Deliver this man to Satan for the destruction of the flesh, *that his spirit may be saved in the day of the Lord Jesus.* (1 Cor 5:5—emphasis mine)

To this collection may be added 2 Corinthians 2:5-11, even if the individual referred to there is not the same one who appears in 1 Corinthians 5:5.

But if any one has caused pain, he has caused it not to me, but in some measure—not to put it too severely—to you all. For such a one this punishment by the majority is enough; so you should rather turn to forgive and comfort him, or he may be overwhelmed by excessive sorrow. So I beg you to reaffirm your love for him. For this is why I wrote, that I might test you and know whether you are obedient in everything. Any one whom you forgive, I also forgive. What I have forgiven, if I have forgiven anything, has been for your sake in the presence of Christ, to keep Satan from gaining the advantage over us; for we are not ignorant of his designs.

The principle of restoration remains intact here. The end of church discipline is not punishment or permanent restriction but rather reconciliation and full restoration.

Even the stern words of 2 Thessalonians 3:6–15 have primary goals of repentance and restoration:

Now we command you, brethren, in the name of our Lord Jesus Christ, that you keep away from any brother who is living in idleness and not in accord with the tradition that you received from us. . . . Now such persons we command and exhort in the Lord Jesus Christ to do their work in quietness and to earn their own living. . . . If any one refuses to obey what we say in this letter, note that man, and have nothing to do with him, that he may be ashamed. Do not look on him as an enemy, but warn him as a brother. (vv. 6, 12, 14–15)

Finally, the classic text of Galatians 6:1–5 should be mentioned also.

Brethren, if a man is overtaken in any trespass, you who are spiritual should restore him in a spirit of gentleness. Look to yourself, lest you too be tempted. Bear one another's burdens, and so fulfil the law of Christ. For if any one thinks he is something, when he is nothing, he deceives himself. But let each one test his own work, and then his reason to boast will be in himself alone and not in his neighbor. For each man will have to bear his own load.

There is no incident in the New Testament of a church-imposed sanction that remained in force throughout the lifetime of a believer.

If the case of Ananias and Sapphira is appealed to as an example of irremediable consequences (namely, death) being imposed by church discipline, several points can be made. First, the incident in Acts 5:1-11 is certainly an extraordinary situation and not to be seen as normative for the church. Second, the case of Ananias and Sapphira was not a case of church discipline. It was God, not man, who intervened. Irremediable consequences remain his prerogative. Third, there is considerable doubt that this passage or its possible counterpart, the "sin which is mortal" of 1 John 5:16, refers to Christians at all.

The New Testament rule is that God changes believers, he doesn't kill them. But even if they were believers in these passages, once again such an ultimate consequence is in the hands of God, not the brotherhood. This should be noted even in the light of that solemn passage in 1 Corinthians 11:30 where abuses at the communion table provoked an obvious judgment of God: "That is why many of you are weak and ill, and some have died."

A strong case can be made in this Corinthian passage that those who had died were those who had taken communion in an "unworthy manner"; that is, they were not Christians, and the church had failed to preserve the Lord's Table for believers only. Once again, however, it should be pointed out that it is God not humans who has the prerogative of permanent punishment.

Sanctions imposed by church discipline on those who

were divorced or remarried must be seen as temporary and for the purpose of effecting full repentance, reconciliation and restoration to that body of believers which is the local church.

Facing Consequences

It could be argued that forgiveness does not automatically remove a person from the consequence of his or her sin. It is true that both David and Moses were among many who were required by God to accept certain limitations to their service because of their past failures. But again it was God, not humans, who exacted such a harsh penalty. While discipline must be affirmed and maintained in the church, apart from clear moral instruction in the Word of God, we have no right to impose arbitrary restrictions on those who seek to serve the Lord.

On the other hand, in the life of Paul we have strong evidence that God's grace can triumph over sinful consequences, nailing them, as it were, to Christ's cross. Paul saw in the forgiveness of his murderous past the triumph of grace over consequence.

The saying is sure and worthy of full acceptance, that Christ Jesus came into the world to save sinners. And I am the foremost of sinners; but I received mercy for this reason, that in me, as the foremost, Jesus Christ might display his perfect patience for an example to those who were to believe in him for eternal life. (1 Tim 1:15-16)

I am the least of the apostles, unfit to be called an apostle, because I persecuted the church of God. But by the grace of God I am what I am. (1 Cor 15:9-10)

To argue that this was only operative because Paul's sin preceded his salvation is an invitation to think that God's goodness operates differently in the life of the believer than it does in the life of the unbeliever. But Jesus, in telling us that our heavenly Father makes the rain to fall on the just and unjust alike, denies that God "plays favorites" in that way. As we shall see in a moment, it is unwise to lean too heavily on the pre- and post-conversion issue as a justification of how we regard sin in the past life of Christians.

The fact that we all must live with the natural consequences of our past actions is axiomatically correct. "Do not be deceived," the apostle warns. "God is not mocked, for whatever a man sows, that he will also reap" (Gal 6:7). It is a moral law, the law of natural consequences. Romans 1:27 refers to this law when it says that "men [were] committing shameless acts with men and receiving in their own persons the due penalty for their error." It appears that God himself underwrites this law of natural consequence:

> I the LORD your God am a jealous God, visiting the iniquity of the fathers upon the children to the third and the fourth generation of those who hate me. (Ex 20:5)

But the natural consequences that divine providence has woven into the moral order of the universe do not form a fatalistic force. The law of the Spirit of life in Christ Jesus is a higher law. It can free us by God's sovereign grace from many of the natural consequences of life as a sovereign God directs.

Some would argue that when a divorced Christian is not allowed to have a particular ministry in the church, it is a natural consequence of his sin. But it is a mistake to insist that a denial of service in the church is a natural consequence for sin of the kind that Galatians 6 or Romans 1 discusses.

The response of God's people to others' past indiscretions is hardly a "natural consequence" in the purest sense of the word. It may be a direct response to what has happened, that is true—but is the response proper? Consequences that reflect God's moral judgment in the physical universe are things to be concerned with and feared, but consequences which result from the willful decisions of others are quite another matter. Christians are to view themselves as agents of grace, and not as God's executioners in the world. Consequences that arise from prejudice or anger or revenge, or even from a misguided attempt to insure "purity," are hardly God-ordained consequences. The fear of such reactions from God's people should never sway the hand of justice and mercy in the church.

When one holds the belief that prohibiting divorced people from having a particular ministry in the church is a natural consequence of the sin of divorce, one enters a Catch-22 of revolving illogic.

Yosarian, the hero of the novel *Catch-22* (a black comedy by Joseph Heller about the air war in Africa and Italy), did not want to participate in any more Allied bombing missions. He concluded rightly that a man could get killed doing such things as flying over enemy targets and dropping bombs. Unfortunately the only way to get out of such missions was to be judged insane. And, since only insane men would want to fly in bombing missions, the befuddled Yosarian is told that it was obvious that he, Yosarian, who wanted out of flying, was undoubtedly perfectly sane.

Therefore he had to fly.

It was Catch-22. If you were insane you could get out of making those deadly bombing runs, but insane people wouldn't want out. If, on the other hand, you were sane, you would want to get out of flying—but then you couldn't because your desire to get out was perfect proof of your sanity And, as Yosarian was told again and again, only insane people could get out of flying. It all sounded so reasonable, so well ordered, so logical. It also sounded crazy.

With a similar leap into the labyrinth of illogic, churches often thrust the divorced into Catch-22s. In so many words divorced people are told, "One of the terrible consequences of your sin will be the way we are going to treat you when you do sin." Like Yosarian's Catch-22, this sounds logical But it is not. It's a conundrum. But it does not have to be.

More than one observer of the problem of divorced people in the church has indulged the tired metaphor: "A bird with a broken wing will never fly as high again." But who says so? This isn't a psalm of grace by any means! It's difficult to accept the crocodile tears of some who sing about the birds with broken wings when they are the ones who will shoot them down when they do try to fly high again.

Who said that hostility toward divorced people is an iron-clad law of nature? Who drew up these rules? The response of God's people should not be a negative, inevitable consequence of sin. It is supposed to be the beginning of grace.

Divorce, But Never Remarriage?

The fact that divorce is a sin capable of forgiveness and that people who are divorced can be fully restored to the church does not in itself pose a severe problem to some. Yet to those same people, on the other hand, the questions of whether or not a divorced person should ever remarry or whether or not divorced people who do remarry can ever be fully restored to church fellowship and service seem to be almost insurmountable problems.

From our Lord's teaching in Matthew 5 and elsewhere, it is clear that remarriage following an improper divorce—implying, as it does, the act of sexual intercourse—is flagrant adultery. However, far from teaching that such a sin places a person in a continual state of adultery, Jesus teaches that it can furnish proper grounds for breaking the marriage relationship. Moreover, Paul reminds us in 1 Corinthians 7, in the case of a marriage union that has been broken because of desertion, the believer is no longer "bound." Flagrant sexual sin and willful desertion are just causes for the breaking of the marriage bond.

Logic should instruct us that if the marriage bond is dissolved because of flagrant sin, there is no longer a continuing issue of adultery to contend with. How can there be adultery when there is no longer a marriage to transgress?

Whether or not one could legitimately remarry in such situations as listed above, the act of remarriage itself, like the act of divorce, becomes a past moral situation and must be dealt with as a past act and not a continuing "sinful state."

To withhold full participation in the life of the Christian community from a fully contrite and repentant believer because he or she has been divorced and remarried is wrong. It is harmful to sound doctrine. A fully contrite and repentant believer must be received by his or her church just as the Lord of the church has commanded:

> Take heed to yourselves; if your brother sins, rebuke him, and if he repents, forgive him; and if he sins against you seven times in the day, and turns to you seven times, and says, "I repent," you must forgive him. (Lk 17:3-4)

It is true that Paul talks about a "godly grief" as opposed to a "worldly grief" in 2 Corinthians 7:10-11. True repentance is represented in the former. The church must be able to distinguish between true and feigned repentance. Consider Paul's words on this matter.

> Godly grief produces a repentance that leads to salvation and brings no regret, but worldly grief produces death. For see what earnestness this godly grief has produced in you, what eagerness to clear yourselves, what indignation, what alarm, what longing, what zeal, what punishment! At every point you have proved yourselves guiltless in the matter.

A feigned repentance based on some ulterior motive is not uncommon in human affairs. Anyone who has ministered the Word of God in moral matters has run across it. As in every matter of life, wisdom must guide the discerning spiritual leaders who must make decisions in such difficult areas. Jesus' simple and direct words in Luke concerning the Christian's obligation to forgive the repentant must never be diluted by carnal passions of anger and a thirst for revenge. On the other hand, as with all Scripture, spiritual things must be compared with spiritual things. The whole Word of God must shed its light on the understanding on any part of the Word of God.

True repentance in 2 Corinthians 7 is marked by a zealous and earnest desire to resolve the issues in question justly. It involves a willingness to face the consequence of the wrong committed. True repentance brings sorrow to those who are penitent. They are distressed over the wrongs that were done. Moreover, true repentance carries a degree of fear over the fate of those who sin and a certain anger toward the sins committed.

In efforts to preserve a salvation free from works–righteousness, some have unbiblically diluted the Bible's teaching regarding repentance. "According to 1 John 1:9," they say, "we need only to confess our sin, and confession simply means agreeing with God that it is wrong." But repentance means much more than that! According to Acts 5:31 and 11:18, as well as 2 Timothy 2:25, repentance is a gift from God.[2] It engages not only the mind, but the will and the emotions as well. Repentance involves the whole person. Spiritual leaders who direct the decisions of the church must understand this and know how to detect true repentance.

In any case, whether there is repentance or not, whether forgiveness is sought or not, when people unlawfully end their marriage and then remarry, they are guilty of adultery. However, they are most certainly not living in a perpetual state of adultery.

It is obvious that the church must do everything in its power to prevent marriages that are contrary to sound biblical teaching. This is yet another side of its mandated role to be a moral arbiter in the lives of its members. Marriages made contrary to the counsel of God's Word are serious acts of rebellion and cannot be allowed to sit outside of the process of discipline that God's Word has established.

If a divorced person remarries contrary to the teaching of Scripture, that person is guilty of sin and must be disciplined according to the New Testament pattern. But the problem becomes somewhat more complex when a professed believer admits personal wrongdoing. What is the church to do in the light of true repentance? The answer is obvious—it must proclaim Christ's forgiveness and model that forgiveness in its own relationships with the penitent party.

In the matter of remarriage, a final consideration should be raised. It is the comfortable practice of many to commit a flagrantly sinful act and then, conveniently, to become "converted." Following the analogy of the "new creature" passage of 2 Corinthians 5:17, and the doctrine of regeneration on the whole, some Christians find it easier to excuse everything and "start over again" than to wade into the tedium of moral complexities. But at times this is nothing more than antinomianism. What is needed is not an escape clause called "conversion," but serious biblical thinking and sound and courageous moral judgment. The response "But now I am a Christian" is not a blank check allowing one to walk away from the moral obligations of the past.

There are times when one can legitimately walk away from past moral obligations. The Christian, for example, may certainly find release from a marriage that harbors an immoral, abusive, deceitful or deserting spouse. One need not be bound in such matters. Therefore certain bonds, bonds that once justly held a believer in the past, can be nullified.

Conversely, however, it is quite possible that a bond from a pre-Christian life can remain in force even after salvation.

This appears to be the undeniable implication of Paul's letter to Philemon where the apostle attempts to obtain the remission of certain moral obligations that still exist for Onesimus even after his conversion.

This is the truth behind the "corban" issue of Mark 7:9-13, where someone is attempting to undo prior obligations by pleading, to no avail, a higher, present "spiritual" priority.

The fact is that certain bonds made even after conversion may be annulled, and likewise certain bonds brought into the Christian life from a non-Christian past may still be in force. Once again the judgment of the local church is needed to sort through complexities of this nature.

The Question of Christian Service

The question of service in the local church can be approached from two sides. First, there is the undeniable fact that Christian service in the church, according to the gifts which the Holy Spirit has imparted to every believer, is not merely a privilege—it is a critical imperative. Christians are not left with an option in this matter. We must serve one another and, having been equipped, we must "do the work of the ministry."

The question then of the role of the divorced and remarried in the church has a more immediate focus than first meets the eye. The ministry that divorced Christians are to have in the local church is a question of discipleship. The local church must face the issue of the role of divorced people in the church as part of its response to the Lord's Great Commission. Regardless of the past, if divorced and remarried Christians are now part of the local church and are professing Christians, they must have avenues of service within that church.

There is also the clear teaching of Scripture to consider in the wake of any sinful situation. We must seek restoration (Gal 6:1; Jas 5:19-20; 2 Cor 2:5-11). Any exclusion from service in the church must be considered in the light of the effect such an exclusion will have on the restorative process.

Sadly, it is true that overly scrupulous prohibitions can cause false guilt and nonproductive remorse. So Paul counsels that those who are disciplined and repent should be forgiven and comforted lest they "be overwhelmed by excessive sorrow" (2 Cor 2:7). Overly harsh discipline may even open up avenues for Satanic attack on the brother or sister who has fallen but is truly seeking restoration. Paul warns every church "to keep Satan from gaining the advantage over us." In the matter of restoring one who had fallen in sin we must not be "ignorant of [Satan's] designs" (2 Cor 2:11).

On the other hand, one's response to biblically correct discipline may demonstrate true and heartfelt repentance more than anything else. The situation must be handled sensitively with prayer and serious deliberation. What a fallen but now repentant brother may or may not do in the church will have lasting instructional impact, not only on that brother or sister, but on the entire church as well.

There can be no restriction imposed on divorced or remarried believers in their service within the church according to the Word of God. With adequate time for observation, with careful control and biblical supervision, with clear teaching to the entire congregation regarding sin, righteousness and judgment, this position can be main-

tained in the life of the church. If this is done, the grace of God and the true balance of biblical holiness and compassion will be affirmed by the entire church. Any attempt to place lasting restrictions on repentant believers' service in the assembly would be wrong. It is also counterproductive to the biblically stated end of all church discipline—repentance and restoration.

It should also be remembered that church discipline not only corrects the errant but affirms the innocent. Those who have been sinned against in the question of divorce need vindication by God's people. It hardly seems supportive to shackle the innocent with prohibitions and lifelong restrictions. It is a little like adding insult to injury and is certainly not in keeping with a scriptural model of discipline.

Leadership

It must be acknowledged, however, that not every kind of service in the church is mandated to every believer. It is not imperative that every believer be in a position of leadership, for example. It is necessary, in fact, that leadership be restricted to those who demonstrate the highest character and are acknowledged to possess the gifts needed for leadership in the assembly. Any superficial survey of the pastoral epistles will reveal this.

Because of this, many suggest that divorced people should be disqualified from full-time ministry or from the highest offices of the church, be it the office of elder, deacon or trustee, depending on church structures. There is very little direct Scripture that supports this suggestion, though some have attempted to read this into a few isolated texts.

The Husband of One Wife

A brief survey of the major commentaries on the pastoral epistles (1, 2 Timothy and Titus) will quickly convince anyone that a surprising number of interpretations cluster about the simple words, "the husband of one wife."[3] On a closer inspection we can understand why this is so. We first encounter the phrase in 1 Timothy 3:2 where it stands second in a list of fifteen moral requirements for the office of bishop or "overseer."[4] All of the requirements are fairly straightforward with only minor questions concerning their meaning—all, I should say, except one. The meaning of the phrase "the husband of one wife" is, to use the words of one contemporary writer, "impossible to understand simply from the words involved."[5]

If we are to understand the phrase at all, we must do so by being instructed from the immediate context since, the meaning of the specific text itself is unclear. Furthermore, we should interpret the phrase not only from the immediate context of 1 Timothy 3:1-7, but also from the broader context of the New Testament's teaching on marital ethics in general and church leadership in particular.

One final introductory observation should be made. Logic alone argues convincingly that the moral requirements listed in 1 Timothy 3:1-7 are not extraordinarily demanding. They are best seen as general moral requirements which God would desire of any believer. They are applicable to the general population of the Christian community as well as to its leaders. In fact it would not be difficult to match each of the requirements in 1 Timothy 3:1-7 with a counterpart New Testament teaching obligating every believer to such behavior. In short, Paul is saying, "If these qualities are to be true of Christians in general, they must certainly be true of Christian leaders."[6] Whatever the phrase "husband of one wife" does mean, it should not be seen as an extraordinary "higher standard" since no such standards exist in this passage.

All fifteen moral requirements of 1 Timothy 3:1–7 are good for every believer to adopt. In fact, it would be a sin to behave contrary to any one of them. Exceptions might be made for two of the fifteen—the requirement for elders to be "apt teachers," and the warning that elders should not be "new converts."

Certainly not every believer is to be a teacher, and no believer can avoid being young at least once in his or her Christian life. Such things are not sinful. But these two requirements are unique from the others in that they are clearly marked out with regard to their utilitarian impact on the assembly.

The other thirteen requirements are absolute moral requirements. Paul states them without any direct application to their immediate use in the church. The application of these thirteen absolute moral requirements to the life of the church may be obvious. The insistence that those who would be elders must manage their own homes and children well are examples of this. Certainly such moral qualities have implied benefits to the life of the church, but only by application. So it can be seen that thirteen of the fifteen requirements in the passage in question are clearly moral absolutes. They can be shown in other passages to be binding on every believer, not merely upon the leadership.

Going beyond this, however, it is not difficult to discover

the absolute moral requirements behind the two simple instructions requiring elders to be apt to teach and warning them of the dangers of a novice. They too can be universalized and made applicable to the Christian community at large. In so doing we can demonstrate why Paul put them in this list for our instruction through the upright, moral lives of the bishops.

The requirement that an elder should be an apt teacher can be universalized by the obvious observation that no teaching in the church should be inept. It would be wrong to teach any other way in the church than aptly since the church is to be the "pillar and ground of the truth."

As far as the requirement for maturity, it is easily universalized by saying that no one should aspire to church leadership without the seasoning of experience, because a respected position in the church is too great a temptation to a young person's pride. No Christian should be vain.

All Christians, then, should aspire to "rightly divide the Word of God" and seek to ensure a secure grip on the truths of the gospel. Moreover, all believers should press toward the attainment of mature attitudes and understanding in the things of the Lord. In this way even the two requirements of 1 Timothy 3:1-7, which seem restricted only to leaders, become universally applicable to the moral desires of all God's people.

It would be a mistake, then, to see the fifteen requirements of 1 Timothy 3:2-7 as being "for bishops only." The bishop, in his morally exemplary role, is standing in for all of us. In this light, if we say, for example, that the phrase "husband of one wife" means bishops must not remarry (for whatever reasons), we are saying that it is better that no believer remarry.

If we deny that the moral qualifications for the office of bishop in 1 Timothy 3:1-7 have a direct impact on every church member's life, we begin a downward slide toward the unacceptable intrusion of the double standard into the life of the church. It is morally dangerous to hold that there is one standard of morality for those in leadership and another, lower standard for the rest of the church.

The various interpretations of the phrase "husband of one wife" can be grouped into five basic categories.[7] We will consider each possibility separately.

Possibility 1: "The husband of one wife" means he must not be a bachelor. According to A. E. Humphries, the early Greek church demanded that their priests be married, and forced them to resign their office if their wife should die. This is hardly what Paul means. It would be difficult to imagine Paul, most probably a bachelor himself, who extolled the virtues of celibacy in 1 Corinthians 7, to turn around and forbid high church offices to those who might follow his advice. Nevertheless, some do hold this view.

I remember early in my own ministry being counseled to discourage a particular bachelor in our church from seeking to be a deacon because Scripture insisted that deacons too must be "husbands of one wife." I remember this because, at the time, I felt this to be a particularly novel slant to extend the phrase in question to refer to those who had never married. Unfortunately, I was to encounter this view again.

Possibility 2: "The husband of one wife" means he must

not be polygamous. This is an extremely popular view among many Bible students.[8] In the first place, it keeps one from the rather arbitrary introduction of the question of divorce into the picture. Also it takes a very simple and straightforward view of the phrase "one wife." However, this is probably not what the phrase "the husband of one wife" means, for at least three reasons.

First, the New Testament world was not patriarchal Palestine. Polygamy, as an institution, was extremely rare in the Jewish and Roman world of the first century.[9] For one thing, it would be a rather expensive proposition. Furthermore, the Roman world around the time of the Empire was growing increasingly fond of the Stoic ideal of monogamy. Whether this reflected simple ascetic, sociopolitical or basic economic concerns, it is still established that monogamy was in ascendancy. As one commentator observed, "Polygamy was such a rare feature of pagan society that such a prohibition would function as a near irrelevancy."[10]

Second, a statement warning against polygamy would not only be socially irrelevant but morally redundant. It would be as unnecessary as it would be painfully obvious, and comparable to Paul reminding us that bishops shouldn't murder.[11] A prohibition against the evil of polygamy should go without saying in the New Testament. And, as far as the phrase "the husband of one wife" is concerned, it probably did.

Finally, if there are a few isolated instances of polygamy in Paul's world, there is certainly no instance of polyandry (one wife having many husbands). Yet, if the phrase, "the husband of one wife" refers to polygamy, then its counterpart in 1 Timothy 5:9 ("the wife of one man") must be a command against polyandry. But it is best to understand that neither phrase is speaking to the question of multiple husbands or wives.

Possibility 3: "The husband of one wife" means he must not remarry after the death of his first wife. Though not a popular view today, it is not, however, unheard of.[12] This view is as old as the second century. The Montanist separatists held to it, as did Tertullian, Origen and other Christian writers. But the earliest Christian writers outside the New Testament seem to reject such a proposition.[13] Paul certainly did. Unless one makes these qualifications a "higher standard" for bishops only, Paul's teaching regarding all believers in Romans 7:1-3 should prove conclusive.

> Do you not know, brethren—for I am speaking to those who know the law—that the law is binding on a person only during his life? Thus a married woman is bound by law to her husband as long as he lives; but if her husband dies she is discharged from the law concerning the husband. Accordingly, she will be called an adulteress if she lives with another man while her husband is alive. But if her husband dies she is free from that law, and if she marries another man she is not an adulteress.

There is nothing morally disqualifying for a Christian to remarry after the death of a spouse. The phrase "the husband of one wife" falls within a list of moral qualifications. Certainly there is nothing immoral about having a spouse who dies.[14]

Possibility 4: "The husband of one wife" means he must not remarry after being divorced from a spouse. As we observed earlier, it seems rather arbitrary to bring the somewhat narrow question of divorce into this rather wide open phrase. There is nothing either in the context, syntax or grammar of 1 Timothy 3 that even hints that a concern over the question of divorce is on the apostle's mind. As one observer put it, "Second marriage is not contemplated and rejected; it does not come into the picture at all."[15]

Furthermore, if there are certain instances where a marriage bond can be dissolved and remarriage take place without moral sin, then the broader context of the biblical ethic governing marriage does not compel us to read divorce into this phrase either.

In order to argue that the phrase "the husband of one wife" prohibits church leaders from remarrying after a divorce, one would have to assert either that there is a double standard erected by Scripture which applies to church leaders but not to the common laity, or that there are no legitimate grounds for divorce and remarriage in the Scripture at all.

Of course, if a double standard is being erected here, then perhaps divorce is what's being referred to in the phrase in question. But it should be noted that this is not a "higher" standard, since there is nothing low about the option of remarriage if God's Word permits it. It would not be a "higher" option at all, just another one.

It is difficult to see how the erection of a higher ethical standard for a church leader would ever allow that leader to function fully as a moral example for the flock. If a leader has separate standards, by definition those measures will not apply to his or her flock; and the flock will not feel compelled to aspire to a standard they feel is beyond them.

If the phrase "husband of one wife" means having a past free from any moral problems in the area of marriage, then do the other fourteen requirements carry the same demands for a past absolutely free of sin in their particular domain? Must we then not only ask "is the person a drunkard" but also "has the person ever been drunk?"[16] If we begin to view these fifteen requirements as absolute and extending indefinitely backward into any potential leader's past, we then must not only ask "is the person dignified?" we must also ask if he or she ever behaved in an undignified manner.

The moral qualifications for church leadership describe the thrust of a man's life now. It is completely unwarranted to use the phrase "husband of one wife" as a rationale for making the marital past a unique moral concern different in kind from all other moral behavior. The phrase "husband of one wife," like all the other moral requirements in the passage, focuses on one's present state of conduct.

Possibility 5: "The husband of one wife" means marital fidelity. The New English Bible translates the phrase *mias gynaikos andra* courageously and best: "faithful to his wife." This rendering best reflects both the immediate moral context which speaks of the moral thrust of a man's life in the present and the general concern of the New Testament doctrine regarding marriage: "Husbands, love your wives."

In the words of Ronald A. Ward:

A husband should love his wife. In so doing he loves himself, for husband and wife are one. When a man has one wife there is a community with two members who in a deep and real sense are one. Paul was thinking of a man

142

at the time of his candidature for office. The appropriate questions would be: "Is he married?" "Does his marriage work?" "Does it fulfill the ideal of marriage?" If it does, the two are one and in particular the man is husband of one wife.[17]

The phrase "the husband of one wife" is best seen as descriptive of marital fidelity.[18] Though early efforts were possibly made outside the New Testament to connect this phrase to the issue of remarriage, it was not until the third century that a majority of Christians began to take such an interpretation seriously.[19] Even then questions of divorce did not enter the picture at all. The earliest considerations in this regard were that bishops should follow a higher (double) standard and be different from the common person in that they should never remarry after the death of their first spouse. As stated above, this view is not supported by the Scripture.

Others view the phrase as opposing polygamy, but as we have observed, this is hardly a pressing New Testament concern. Furthermore, the question of divorce and church leadership does not even enter the parameters of this phrase in any logical connection. The phrase "husband of one wife" does not describe one's past "track record" at the altar. Rather it seems to say that God's people in general must revere and sanctify marriage. Leaders in particular (because of their example) should be noted for their faithful, loving devotion to the woman who is their wife.[20]

Fred and the 800-Pound Gorilla

I'd like to tell you about a dear friend of mine named Fred.

In many ways his life's story reminds me of the old joke about the 800-pound gorilla. Remember it?

Question: "Where does an 800-pound gorilla sleep?"

Answer: "Anywhere it wants to."

Bad joke? Possibly. But it has great potential for illustrating the work of God.

Question: "What can God do?"

Answer: "Anything he wants to."

(I hope those more conversant with the deeper philosophical issues of God's nature and his works will allow that last statement to stand. It was meant to affirm God's sovereign grace, not to diminish free agency or to attribute a capricious nature to God. Given the perfect balance between God's nature and his will, it's true: God can do anything he wants to do. And that's what he did in Fred's life.)

Fred was a Christian from childhood. He was raised in a Christian home and he always had a deep love for his mother and his father. It was not too difficult for Fred, even as a teen-ager, to follow the God of his father. And so he did in sincerity.

Fred showed great creative promise in his school work and went off to college to receive a fine education at a prestigious university. Fred did quite well. His promise bore early fruit as he began to do work related to his intended profession. His life continued to take happy directions when Fred met, fell in love with and finally married a girl who shared his faith.

After college, Fred took an academic post and also took occasional professional contracts in the private sector. He excelled in both worlds. Soon Fred's abilities began to show even more. It was obvious that he had significant administrative qualities. His academic post expanded with increased responsibilities. He also served his church as a deacon.

One day Fred came home after a typical madhouse day at the office. Though the job was demanding, it was exciting. There was so much to do, but there was so much that had been done. Fred felt a great deal of satisfaction. He was able to do exactly what he wanted to do.

But the roof fell in that day. Fred's wife greeted him that evening with a cold and final, non-negotiable announcement. "I'm leaving you," she said in a firm, dispassionate voice.

"I just don't want to be your wife anymore," she admitted when Fred asked her why. She repeated it when he pleaded with her to seek counsel with him. She didn't retreat. She didn't advance. She held her ground.

"I'm leaving you!"

No matter how he pleaded, no matter who counseled them, his wife remained adamant and implacable. What could he do? He didn't let her go. He watched her go.

Letting Go

Fred's church was horrified. Divorce was simply unheard of (though, sadly, it was being heard of more and more). His parents were grief stricken. Though they lived over five hundred miles north of him, they tried to help their son all they could. But what could anyone do? Fred's wife had left him, and no one could *do* anything. Shortly after the divorce, his wife married again. She married a man who was from out of state. Probably a nonbeliever.

What was worse was that Fred was also horrified with *himself.* He didn't believe in divorce either—but now he was divorced. As so many mistakenly do, Fred read the Scripture wrongly. Where it says "God hates divorce," Fred read, "God hates the divorced." And now he was one of them.

In confusion, in despair, in anger and even in shame, Fred slipped slowly from the company of Christians. He drifted from his believing friends. Quietly, he let his church attendance dwindle down and die.

This silent retreat, a sort of nonviolent, passive resistance, is a common tactic among Christians who have been divorced. The local church, which should be a place to run *to,* becomes a thing to run *from.* Usually this retreat is not an act of angry protest, but a hesitant course taken by those who are confused and ashamed. But it does gather a certain momentum as it slides one down the path of least resistance.

It was the gathering twilight of the flower children, the era of water pipes, beads and VW vans, and Fred's hair began to grow down upon his shoulders about as quietly, slowly, but inexorably as he had vacated his church, his Christian friends and his Christian lifestyle. Fred was on a journey somewhere east of Eden. The mark God gave him (so he thought) was a divorce decree.

Fred experienced what a surprising number of other fundamentalists were discovering in the days of the hippie movement. There was a strange compatibility between the Bible-believing "rock-ribbed fundy" and the flower-waving, psychedelic sweetness of the "street people." Maybe it was the idealism, maybe the individualism; maybe it was something you and I will never understand. But it was something Fred began to live.

To be sure, in the counterculture of the early seventies there was a lot of hostility to the gospel. But more often than not, it was the rebellious actions of the counterculture and not its thinking that was in conflict with the gospel. The stand-off was usually behavioral, not ideological. As with so many people in those turbulent times, Fred never denied his faith, he just stopped living it. Still, the call of God, though distant and remote, tugged at his heart. At times, the wistful, homeward look of the prodigal would pass over Fred's face.

After several years, Fred met a rather remarkable young woman. She was by no means a believer, but she was an honest and faithful person who, to Fred's amazement, was deeply in love with him. Fred knew it was wrong. But often knowledge isn't enough. Besides, he loved this young woman and saw goodness, honesty and loyalty in her character—qualities that were often sadly lacking in the lives of those who glibly called themselves born-again believers.

Fred knew it was wrong. But since his own life was lacking a spiritual base, why should his marriage be any different? The last Christian he was "yoked" with broke his heart and shattered his life. Besides, Fred didn't want an argument, he wanted a wife and a family.

Fred knew it was wrong. But he went ahead and married an unbeliever. It was about this time that the 800-pound gorilla paid Fred a visit. He and his wife were visiting his parents one holiday. Fred's dad, never accused of being overly delicate, confronted his new daughter-in-law with the gospel. His dad pressed the case for the lordship of Jesus.

Fred couldn't deny the gospel, and he knew that what his dad was saying was true, but he winced at the pain of the inner personal conflict this witness was causing him.

Fred's wife listened. And, after a time of first being offended, then confused, then guilty, she called on the Lord Jesus Christ to be her personal Savior and Lord. It's called "conversion." Fred saw his wife come into the kingdom of God. But where was he?

Fred saw the face of the 800-pound gorilla. Fred felt all the hurt and resentment, all the love he still held for God and the cold fear of yet another betrayal welling up within him. Fred loved God. He knew he was his child. And in this wondrous act of mercy, the saving of his new bride, Fred saw a clear confirmation of how much God loved him and desired his fellowship.

"Neither do I condemn thee" seemed written all across the sky.

Coming Home

Fred turned back to the Lord. And, as is only right, Fred and his wife sought out a fellowship of Christian brothers and sisters. I am deeply thankful to God that they chose our church.

About ten years passed, and Fred and his wife were showing themselves to be very serious in the matter of building a Christian home. At that time they had two children (a third was to come later). They were hungry to learn God's Word. Both of them enriched the church life with a loving concern for people.

Fred stayed busy, but even in the midst of a successful

academic life he found time to serve our fellowship sacrificially. Fred repeatedly demonstrated gifts of teaching and evangelism. Having been there himself, Fred had a deep concern for those who felt "burned" by life. He was a compassionate counselor. He didn't duck the hard facts, but shared them with empathy. People in trouble often sought Fred out.

When sharing his testimony, Fred never avoided the responsibility for the failure of his first marriage, nor did he justify his period of rebellion. He extolled the grace of God and challenged us to be faithful to the God who was so faithful to him.

In short, his house was in order, his family was in submission, he was well thought of both in and outside the church, and he held the doctrines of God with a clear conscience. Fred often showed a definite aptness to teach. I think you know what I'm talking about. This man was an elder.

Some time before this I had come to the strong conviction that the ethical commands of Scripture, though absolutely binding on us, are not static, once-for-all rules attained absolutely and then held everafter without wavering.

God's call to ethical behavior is not a grocery list to be ticked off as the goods, item by item, are tossed into our shopping cart. Nor were God's ethical commands intended to describe the punctilious attainments of our life. ("Today I'm working on patience. When I get that down, I'm going to move on to joy.") This would make God's moral requirements appear to be set forth like so many merit badges to be won. On the contrary, God's moral requirements describe the quality of the day-by-day ebb and flow of life as God wants it to be lived.

The qualities of an elder are not entities to be achieved once and for all, but rather they are lived out daily, they are sought after continually. With regard to moral conduct, the elder does not rest on some supposed higher standard of behavior. Like all of us, the elder seeks to be obedient to the lordship of Christ and the moral requirements of God's Word.

Into the crucible of every believer's life, amid the ingredients of serious obedience to God in spite of the inevitable impurities of sin, are lavishly poured the mercy and forgiveness and restorative power of God. It's called grace.

Restoration

On the strength of their ten years of solid Christian growth, I sat down with Fred and his wife one day and asked them if they would consider a call for Fred to be an elder in our church. Their first reaction was fear. Many Christians feel divorce disqualifies them from church leadership for life. They didn't feel that idea was consistent with God's grace and neither did I, but still they did not want to be the source of controversy. They didn't know whether they were willing to endure the possible storm that might arise over Fred becoming an elder. After prayer and thought, Fred agreed to be nominated as a fellow elder, if the other elders were willing.

Next I gave a clear exposition to the congregation of Fred's past and the doctrine of Scripture concerning church office (a presentation much like the one I have written here). Fred's name was then placed in nomination to be an elder of our church. No one voted no.

The issue challenged many in their own thinking. Our fellowship takes both Scripture and its leadership quite seriously. But at the bottom line, both the logic of God's Word and the manifest call of God in Fred's life drove them to acknowledge God's gracious and sovereign will.

It's been over four years now that Fred has served as an elder. In that time the church has passed through some of the toughest problems and decisions of its short life. In the face of all of this, Fred has stood with his fellow elders shoulder to shoulder. He's been a source of great strength for us all.

In looking back on the selection of Fred to be an elder, I have from time to time wondered at how it progressed with so little opposition, since the prejudice against divorced leaders in the church is so strong among many good and godly people. But in Fred's case at least, arguing against his particular suitability to be an elder would have been like taking on an 800-pound gorilla.

The Leader's Family Life

Going beyond this contested phrase, the Pauline charge that a leader in the church should "rule his own family well" is also appealed to as a prohibition against the divorced serving in leadership. But it would be very difficult to narrow the focus of that charge to such a restrictive issue as divorce alone. Certainly the passage has much broader implications. Furthermore, it is a description of a present situation and not an indictment of any past difficulty.

We note further that all the biblical requirements for church office describe the *thrust* of a person's life, not the fact that one perfectly and continually embodies such high characteristics. What parent has not rightly questioned that he or she has ruled the house well? What spouse has not had to confess the neglect of his or her marriage at one time or another? The requirements of leadership as touching the domestic life are reflective of intentions and purposes for the present and the future, not simply the attainments of the past. Indeed, the past must be considered, but primarily as it indicates the present direction of life.

Ordination and the Double Standard

Concerning the issue of divorce, remarriage and ordination, much more heat than light has been generated lately in evangelical circles. Perhaps one consideration should concern us more than any other in the present debate. Few people have been willing to examine thoroughly the implications of a double standard in the church regarding leadership.

If the clergy operate on a *higher* standard than the laity, it logically follows that they then operate on a *different* standard. All at once we create a tension between pastor and people that holds great danger. If the clergyman is held apart from the congregation, he ceases to be the role model that Scripture demands of all leaders. He is different. He marches to the tune of a different drummer and his life, intended to be a strong force for moral instruction, becomes irrelevant to the laity. A higher standard all too quickly becomes an *other* standard—one that is at best an irrelevant standard, and at worst, one that is contemptible in the eyes of the layman.

Though it is dangerous to appeal too confidently to history, we do have a fine example of the danger of the double standard. The Catholic priesthood should serve as a warning about erecting double standards in the church. In the Catholic church, it ultimately led to the tyranny of one group over another—clergy over lay. It also clearly contributed to terrible moral decline in the church until the Reformation restored the concept of the believer priest and the continuum between all peoples in the eyes of God.

Some have appealed to the Old Testament notion of priesthood for an analogy to the New Testament pastor/teacher in order to defend a double standard within the church between the clergy and the laity. But that is unwise in that it tends to obscure the priesthood of all believers, which is the true antitype that stands behind the symbolism of the Old Testament priesthood. I fear that a Pandora's box of problems has unwittingly been opened upon the church because of this misunderstanding.

Particularly over the issue of divorce and remarriage, some have employed a rather emotional rhetoric with calls for a "higher standard" for our church leadership. This tragically carries a hidden agenda of dualism. It should be rejected. In its place should be a call for the *highest* standard of leadership in the church. A standard which, thanks to the grace of God in Christ Jesus, is attainable to all, just as full and free forgiveness is attainable to all.

It is true that James 3:1, if read uncritically, could be seen as an admission of a double standard. "Let not many of you become teachers, my brethren, for you know that we who teach shall be judged with greater strictness." But a closer reading will confirm that the standard remains the same. The intensity is heightened, but this is done along the established logical lines of Jesus' teaching when he says that the judgment we give is the judgment we get (Mt 7:1-2). The principle of reciprocity assures the teacher that he will be held to the strictest accountability. So James, in sound Midrashic form, gives his warning. He is not admitting to a double standard, but he is cautioning against presumption. Ultimately leadership in the church does not rest on the human attainment of a standard of purity but rather it rests upon the gifts and calling of God.

In light of this, it is not our sin that defines our service in the church, but rather it is the call of God in our lives. The call of God in the life of believers for whom Christ died should not be shackled with word games, or Pharisaisms, or even sincere, if misguided, attempts at piety.

A New Response to Divorce

Growing up in, shall we say, progressive Southern California in the forties and fifties, I was not brought face to face with divorce until one of my junior-high-school friends informed me that his parents were seeking a divorce. My oldest son, on the other hand, growing up in the rural area of the southern Bible Belt thirty years later, knew at least five playmates who came from broken homes before he entered kindergarten. With all manner of statistical fluctuations notwithstanding, divorce is an epidemic that is sweeping over our country. Where is the church to fit into this reality?

The pain of unbearable burdens, as Jesus and Peter both observed, is great. The church must not lay such burdens on divorced people. Rather, we should bear one another's burdens and so fulfill the law of Christ. Above all, we must not become contemporary Pharisees who, for the sake of our misguided sense of purity, refuse to share the burdens of others. The church of Jesus Christ must cultivate a greater trust in the forgiveness and redemptive power of Jesus in the lives of the worst sinners. It must develop more confidence in the process of judgment that Jesus has entrusted to it. The church must be willing to make mistakes, take risks and become vulnerable to moralistic criticism in order to bring hope and salvation in Christ to those who have been guilty of destroying their marriages and threatening their very lives.

Such a task is hard, if not impossible. But it seems clearly the way of the cross. If we do not follow it, at best we will become useless to those who need the savor of spiritual teaching. At worst we will become progressively ingrown, talking in a language unknown to those outside and consequently talking only to ourselves, until we have nothing to say to anyone. Eccentricity may be quaint at certain levels, but eccentricity and isolationism among those who have been commanded by God to rescue and to win the world is not acceptable. Our position on divorce and remarriage and our willingness to be fearlessly biblical in the face of serious moral challenges in this day and age may be a test from God proving whether or not any church remains a truly dynamic and viable fellowship in a world hungering for effective church life.

A final plea would be for local churches to begin a thorough reassessment of their accessibility to those who have been or are now going through divorce. The local church should continually re-evaluate its doctrinal position on the entire question of divorce and remarriage as well as its practice of decision making regarding moral problems within the church. The local church should fearlessly and even ruthlessly re-evaluate its positions regarding qualifications for service and leadership within its own ranks.

Hopefully, these processes would result in renewed thinking concerning the plight of the divorced person in our communities. With God's blessing, they may even result in the beginning of dynamic gospel ministries in vast sectors of our community that deeply need to hear the message of Jesus and yet, for one reason or another, have been or have felt disenfranchised from God's redemptive community—the church. The church, however, is for the divorced, the morally scared, the spiritually needy. We must learn how to speak this truth in every language and in every culture, including the multiple mission fields of our own country. We must learn to speak to everyone the words each of us once heard from our Savior: "Come to me, all who labor and are heavy laden, and I will give you rest" (Mt 11:28).

Notes

Chapter 1: Our Long National Nightmare

[1]In 1940 our country saw one divorce occur for every six marriages. Ten years later the divorce rate had risen to 1 in 4 marriages. By the late 1960s, statisticians were projecting that in the coming decade 35 out of every 100 women over the age of thirty in the United States would experience at least one divorce in their lifetime. One in every three marriages had ended in divorce by the early 1970s (Gerald R. Leslie, *The Family in Social Context*, Oxford Press, 1979).

The divorce rate in America has been rapidly advancing from 1962, when there were 413,000 divorces in the U.S., until 1981, when a record 1,213,000 divorces were recorded nationwide (A.P. wire story, 3/7/85). For the present, a slight reversal appears to have set in. The divorce rate actually dropped 6% in 1982. But this is probably an indication of a decline in our country's regard for marriage rather than a sign of any change in our national attitudes about divorce. In other words, the damage may already have been done. Whether or not such damage is irreversible remains to be seen. But there are some alarming indicators that marriage and family life in America have been dealt a devastating blow in a relatively short period of time.

The 1986 Information Please Almanac (Boston: Houghton, Mifflin,

1986) noted that while the percentage of our population between the ages of 20 and 44 (prime marriageable ages) had risen dramatically between 1970 and 1980, the percentage of people between the ages of 20 and 34 who have never married increased significantly as well.

The *Almanac* statistics went on to show that the number of families in the U.S.A. increased on an average of 1.5% per year from 1970 to 1980 while the population of 20 to 44-year-olds increased 5.4% per year. The figures indicate nothing short of a revolution quietly going on in the American conception of marriage and family. Compare the last decade with the ones that preceded it. From 1960 to 1970 the number of families in the U.S.A. increased on the yearly average of 1.4% while the population of 20 to 44-year-olds (again, prime marriageable ages) actually dropped .5% per year. From 1950 to 1960 the rate of family growth increased 1.5% per annum while the population of 20 to 44-year-olds dropped 5.4% per year. From 1940 to 1950 family growth increased 2.2% annually while the population of 20 to 44-year-olds declined an average of 1.3% per year. For thirty years the trend had been for the number of families to increase in the U.S. *even when the population of those of marriageable age decreased.* But in the past decade, when the population of those of marriageable age increased at an unprecedented rate, the rate of family growth remained virtually unaffected.

It is dangerous to generalize regarding such major social trends on the basis of limited numbers and a relatively small amount of time in which to chart their course. However, even the most conservative reaction to the figures available must be a growing conviction that the major child-rearing and human-nurturing institutions in our society—marriage and the family—are passing through an era of enormous instability. The result of this is not statistically observable, but a Christian conscience should be capable of some sound conclusions that the quality of the moral life in our society will suffer as a result of these drastic changes.

[2]A recent study noted that fully 25% of all children raised in the United States today are raised in single-parent families (U.P.I. wire story, 5/15/85). Divorce is a leading contributor to the growing number of "semi-abandoned" children. Social psychologists are only beginning to document the damage this arrangement does to our young.

One such study by the Kettering Foundation was reported on by David Broder of the *Washington Post.* The report showed that 40% of single-parent children can be classified as low achievers in school. They have a higher incidence of sickness, truancy and are twice as likely to drop out of high school before graduation. They are far more likely to become members of the chronically unemployed than children living with two parents (see *International Herald Tribune,* 1/28/86).

Chapter 2: Marriage Was Built to Last

[1]The great Hillel, for example, believed a wife's poor cooking was sufficient grounds for divorce. Akiba felt divorce was justified "even if [the husband] found another fairer than she" (*The Mishnah,* ed. Herbert Danby [Oxford: Oxford University Press, 1933], *Gittin* 9:10, p. 321). Other rabbis "give us repeated lists of the unseemly characteristics of women such as stinginess . . . gossip, bad temper, and the like." Samuel Sandmel, *Judaism and Christian Beginnings* (New York: Oxford University Press, 1978), pp. 194-95.

[2]Hopefully, the careful reader will note the words *illegitimate* and *arbitrary* in considering the breaking of the marriage bond. I will argue that we can, under God's authority, legitimately end a marriage relationship—but this remains for a later discussion.

[3]With regard to the vulnerability of the husbandless woman in Palestine, we need only consider the book of Ruth. Though one thousand years before Christ, the institutions of marriage had changed little among the common people. The vulnerability of both Ruth and Naomi, assumed in the narrative, underscores their terrible plight and Boaz's redemptive goodness. As for the dominance of the male in these matters, Samuel Sandmel said it well: "[In] the Jewish world . . . all rights lay with [the man], and the woman, in a strict sense, had almost none" (Sandmel, *Judaism,* p.193). It is true that Mark 10:12 speaks of the option of the woman divorcing the man, but that was certainly rare in Palestine. One is tempted to consider it as Mark's own expansion, as the Holy Spirit inspired him, for the easier comprehension of his Roman readers.

[4]The awkward final clause of verse 11, "and that the husband should not divorce his wife," is best considered epexegetic. It borrows from the conditions of the previous clause concerning the wife. The conditions placed upon the wife apply in equal force to the more briefly stated instructions to the husband. In short, the husband should not abandon his marriage either, but if he does, he too should remain single or else

be reconciled to his wife. If this is not the force of the final clause, then one is faced with the intolerable assumption that Paul teaches that husbands may do as they wish with regard to remarriage and only the wives are obligated to seek reconciliation. This is certainly not the teaching of this passage!

[5]Though not a prevalent opinion today, from at least Tertullian onward (see *Ad Uxorem, De Exhortatione Castitatis,* and *De Monogamia,* et al.). Some Christians have viewed a refusal to remarry after a spouse's death as being more spiritual than marrying a second time.

[6]Joseph Henry Thayer, *Greek-English Lexicon of the New Testament* (Grand Rapids, Mich.: Baker, 1977), p. 131. See also Büchsel in Kittel's *Theological Dictionary of the New Testament,* vol. 2 (Grand Rapids, Mich.: Eerdmans, 1965), p. 60; and Sandmel, *Judaism,* p. 473, n. 18.

[7]Of course one could argue that it would be possible to write a rather large book on the various understandings of the word *fornication* in this context. Without apology, I decline to do so. At a time when the need for a general understanding of Scripture's teaching on divorce is so desperately apparent, I find myself growing rather impatient with discussions that get bogged down, if not outrightly diverted from the heart of the question, by pursuing the nuances of exegetical esoterica. If the Protestant doctrine of the perspicuity of Scripture has any value and the need for general application of Scripture to the life of the church any merit, there are times when forgoing exhaustive analysis is not only allowable but advisable. The least that can be said about the word *fornication* is that it is sexual sin, and sexual sin of the worst kind. In my opinion, it is not only the least to be said, but at this juncture, is all that need be said.

[8]By "implicit logic" I mean that marriage and divorce is a personal, but not a private matter. Jesus' words are addressed to Christians in community. Marriage, divorce and even adultery are matters of corporate recognition. Likewise, the exception clause is a corporate concern. Jesus sees a corporate verification in operation. He addresses the church. And the church must always decide matters on the basis of clear evidence. Both A. H. McNeile in his *The Gospel According to St. Matthew* (London: MacMillan, 1965), p. 66, and W. C. Allen in *A Critical and Exegetical Commentary on the Gospel According to St. Matthew* (Edinburgh: T.& T Clark, 1907), p. 52, note that the clause probably reflects a Hebrew

term used in technical, forensic matters. McNeile calls the preposition rare. (On the doctrine of establishing all the allegations of moral offense, see Matthew 18:15 and 1 Timothy 5:19.)

[9]The whole of Matthew 5:32 is expressed in the *apodictic* or "if . . . then" form of Jewish case law. These are nonspecific, hypothetical situations. This was a familiar way for Jewish writers to list possible situations and their consequences. The exception clause is all the more remarkable then, because it breaks the strict pattern of this straightforward, near-axiomatic type of saying. In other words, the clause is not only an exception to the logical argument of the passage, it is also an exception to its formal presentation. This makes the exception clause all the more emphatic in the mind of its Jewish readers. Since the form of Matthew 5:32 carries a general, nonspecific, all-things-being-equal tenor to its expression, it tends to flavor the exception clause with the same sense, encouraging the exception to be seen not as a singular occurrence but as a general pattern of behavior. Moreover, the clause appears to be a carefully worded, more abstract circumlocution. It appears to describe behavioral patterns, not single acts, since Matthew uses the more oblique prepositional phrase and not a finite verbal clause such as *ei mei porneuei* ("unless she should commit fornication"). If ever so lightly then, the abstraction of this prepositional phrase, as well as its hypothetical "if . . . then" form which makes it appear as an expression of a general rule if certain situations pertain, suggests that a pattern of immorality is in focus here, not simply a single act.

[10]"Paul wrote to you according to the wisdom given him, speaking of this as he does in all *his letters.* There are some things in them hard to understand, which the ignorant and unstable twist to their own destruction, as they do the *other scriptures*" (2 Pet 3:15-16, emphasis mine).

[11]For example, Ephesians 5:3-5:

> But fornication and all impurity or covetousness must not even be named among you, as is fitting among saints. Let there be no filthiness, nor silly talk, nor levity, which are not fitting; but instead let there be thanksgiving. Be sure of this, that no fornicator or impure man, or one who is covetous (that is, an idolater), has any inheritance in the kingdom of Christ and of God.

[12]"And I say to you: whoever divorces his wife, except for unchastity, and marries another, commits adultery." The disciples said to him, "If such

is the case of a man with his wife, it is not expedient to marry." But he said to them, "Not all men can receive this saying, but only those to whom it is given. For there are eunuchs who have been so from birth, and there are eunuchs who have been made eunuchs by men, and there are eunuchs who have made themselves eunuchs for the sake of the kingdom of heaven. He who is able to receive this, let him receive it" (Mt 19:9–12).

[13]The Institutes of Gaius is a midsecond-century compendium of Roman Imperial Law which accurately reflects the legal mindset of the Roman world in the days of Paul. In lines 9–11 of his First Commentary, Gaius makes this telling observation: "The primary division of the law of persons is this—that all men are either free or slaves. Of freemen again some are 'ingenui' and others 'libertini', those manumitted from lawful slavery (*The Institutes of Gaius and the Rules of Ulpian,* James Muirhead, ed. [Edinburgh: T. & T. Clark, 1880], pp. 4–5). Gaius goes on to distinguish between the term *freemen,* which describes the standing of both the *ingenui* and the *libertini* before the law, and the term *freedmen,* which was simply another word for the *libertini,* denoting the past from which they had been set free.

To the Roman legal mind of the first and second centuries, neither the *ingenui* (men born free, who never had a bond of slavery against them) nor the *libertini* (men who once did have a bond of slavery against them but were manumitted from that slavery) had any standing injunction against the full use of their existing liberty before the law.

It would be most fitting, then, for Paul, who had such a respect for the genius of Roman law, to reflect in his own vocabulary the distinctions of Roman legal thinking when discussing matters of societal importance that required technical precision.

Consequently, I am strongly encouraged to see Paul's use of the word *free* in 1 Corinthians 7 to be influenced by the distinctions of Roman law. The idea of a *freedman* (one of the *libertini*) most certainly lies behind the teaching of 1 Corinthians 7:15, where a brother or sister is no longer said to be "bound" to a departing, unbelieving spouse. It is also the idea behind the use of the word *free* in 1 Corinthians 7:27, where the rhetorical question is asked, "Are you free from a wife?"

Interestingly enough, Paul literally uses the very concept of the *libertini* in his illustration of Christian calling in 1 Corinthians 7:20-24, which strongly indicates that the idea of a freedman was very much on his mind as he wrote this section.

It seems best, then, to see Paul's use of the word *free* in 1 Corinthians 7 to mean one who at one time had a wife but had since been released from the bond of matrimony. Paul apparently had no problem with the remarriage of those who had once been married, provided a lawful setting free had taken place. Thus, in 1 Corinthians 7 it seems best to view those who were said to be "free" from a spouse as those who at one time were *not* free from a spouse, that is to say, those who were at one time married but were now set free by a divorce. And, since they bear the title "free," it seems best to view them as free to remarry. This would be their legal and moral right since, like the freedman, no legal bond would restrain them. The freeman, who was born free and never had an entanglement, and the freedman, who though at one time was entangled but had been set free, were both considered equally "free" before the bar of Roman justice.

Chapter 4: Making the Right Decisions

¹Paul informs us that the small and relatively remote church at Philippi was governed by "bishops and deacons" (Phil 1:1). We should note the plurality of leadership that existed in that small church. In Acts 20:17 we read that Paul "called to him the elders [plural] of the church [singular]." for a meeting at Troas. This earmarked Paul's church-planting ministry from the very beginning, as Acts 14:23 notes at the end of Paul's first missionary journey. "They had appointed elders [plural] for them in every church [singular]." This was not only Paul's personal practice, it was also his pattern for others to follow. "This is why I left you in Crete, that you might . . . appoint elders [plural in every town" (literally "according to a city" or "city by city"—Tit 1:5). Going beyond the ministry of Paul, the apostle Peter refers to "elders" (plural) who tend the "flock of God" (singular) in 1 Peter 5:1-2. The very words of Jesus himself in Matthew 18 seem to display an escalation of involvement from one person, to two or three, and finally to a larger number when it is told to the church. Church leadership is a plural concern. So it seems best that in matters of "binding" and "loosing," a number of church leaders, whatever their title or function, should be involved in the judgment process. In referring to the process of Matthew 18 Jesus speaks in what appears to be an

attempt to define the very smallest number who participate in the decisions described. Nevertheless, he still places his remarks in a corporate setting. "Where two or three are gathered in my name," he says, "there am I in the midst of them" (v. 20).

[2]J. B. Lightfoot, *The Epistle of St. Paul to the Galatians* (Grand Rapids, Mich.: Zondervan, 1968), p. 216.

[3]Fredrick Rendall, *The Expositor's Greek Testament*, ed. W. Robertson Nicoll (Grand Rapids, Mich.: Eerdmans, 1967), p. 189

Chapter 5: The Ministry of Divorced People in a Local Church

[1]Perhaps it is possible to conceive of a situation where both parties are innocent. In war time, for example, false reports of death are tragically commonplace. It is possible for a soldier to be reported dead only to have him emerge, years later, as a prisoner of war. Suppose such a false report of death became the basis for a mistaken remarriage by a wife who was under the false impression that she was a widow. Such anomalous situations, however, would be so rare that any attempt to fashion a general principle to govern them would prove to be absurd. The old legal adage "Hard cases make bad law" holds true here. Such singularities have to be dealt with as they make their extraordinarily rare appearances. Nevertheless, the possibilities do challenge the sensitive advocate of biblical standards to maintain a certain flexibility to the problems of divorce that defy any rigid pattern. This flexibility certainly lies within the capacity of a discerning church which would be able to face extreme and remote possibilities with something more than a strict Talmudic legalism.

[2]"God exalted him at his right hand as Leader and Savior, to give repentance to Israel and forgiveness of sins" (Acts 5:31). "To the Gentiles also God has granted repentance unto life." (Acts 11:18) "God may perhaps grant that they will repent and come to know the truth" (2 Tim 2:25).

[3]The phrase appears three times in the New Testament. 1 Timothy 3:2, concerning bishops *(episkopoi)*: *mias gynaikos andra*. 1 Timothy 3:12, concerning deacons *(diakonoi)*: *mias gynaikos andres*. And Titus 1:6, concerning elders *(presbyteroi)*: *mias gynaikos anēr*. It is best to see the elders and bishops of 1 Timothy 3 and Titus 1 as synonymous. They are two words describing the same church office. (Compare Titus 1:5 with 1:7; and see also 1 Peter 5:1-2.) The phrase *mias gynaikos anēr* means

164

quite literally: "a one-woman man." A similar phrase describing widows is found in 1 Timothy 5:9: *henos andros gynē* ("wife of one husband").

[4]The words Paul uses in this passage are *episkopē* (v. 1), which refers to the office of "overseer," and *episkopos* (v. 2), which refers to the man who holds that office. It can easily be shown that the word *overseer* is interchangeable with the word *elder* in the writings of St. Paul. (Compare, for example, Titus 1:7 where the word *overseer* stands in place of the word *elder* which appeared in Titus 1:5. Both verses refer to the same men.) The bishop-overseers are required to be: (1) above reproach, (2) husbands of one wife, (3) temperate, (4) sensible, (5) dignified, (6) hospitable, (7) apt teachers, (8) no drunkards, (9) not violent, (10) gentle, (11) not quarrelsome, (12) no lovers of money, (13) good home managers, (14) no recent converts and (15) well thought of by outsiders.

[5]Robert Saucy, "Husband of One Wife," *Bibliotheca Sacra* 131 (1974): 229-30.

[6]"St. Paul's usage is not to make laws of a 'higher life' for ministers than for people, but to expect the same laws kept in a way to serve for ensamples to the flock" (A. E. Humphries, *The Epistle of Timothy and Titus*, The Cambridge Bible [Cambridge: University Press, 1897]). See also Lock, *I.C.C.* on 1 Timothy 3:2; and Dibelius and Conzelmann, *The Pastoral Epistles* (Philadelphia: Fortress Press, 1972).

[7]I am indebted to the very lucid discussion of 1 Timothy 3:2 found in Ronald A. Ward's *1 & 2 Timothy & Titus* (Waco, Texas: Word, 1974). His clear and uncomplicated discussion of the interpretive options of verse 2 is both thorough and concise.

[8]This view is rarely held by modern scholars though Humphries (see n. 6, above) does see polygamy referred to here.

[9]A. T. Hansen argues that even though it may be possible to document an occasional incident of polygamy in the Jewish world of Paul's day, such an occurrence would merely be the rare exception that proved the rule of monogamy. *(The Pastoral Epistles,* The New Century Bible Commentary [Grand Rapids, Mich.: Eerdmans, 1982]. Lock, Dibelius-Conzelmann et al. also observe this often overlooked fact.)

[10]Gordon Fee, *1 and 2 Timothy, Titus* (San Francisco: Harper and Row, 1984).

[11]Ward, *1 & 2 Timothy & Titus,* p. 55.

[12]Surprisingly, J. N. D. Kelly holds this rather anachronistic position. See

A Commentary on the Pastoral Epistles (London: Adams & Charles Black, 1963).

[13]The Shepherd of Hermas, possibly a first-century work, indicates that some teaching was afoot claiming that it was a sin to remarry after the death of a spouse, but this is soundly rejected. "If, sir," said I, "a wife, or, on the other hand, a husband, die, and the survivor marry, does the one who marries commit sin?" "He does not sin," said he, "But, if he remain single he gains for himself more exceeding honor and great glory with the Lord, but if he marry he does not sin" (Mandate 4, c. 4). Interestingly, the "exceeding honor and great glory with the Lord" correlates nicely with Paul's words in 1 Timothy 3:1. If this is so, then Hermas may be saying that it is a good thing if an elder/bishop remains single (per Paul in 1 Corinthians 7), but if an elder/bishop remarries "he does not sin." In any case, the conviction that it was wrong to remarry after the death of a spouse has little support before the end of the second century.

[14]Robert Saucy, "Husband of One Wife," p. 230: "The Scriptures nowhere forbid or even suggest as morally questionable remarriage after the death of a spouse."

[15]Ward, *1 & 2 Timothy & Titus,* p. 55.

[16]Saucy argues this ably in Bib. Sac.

[17]Ward, *1 & 2 Timothy & Titus,* p. 55.

[18]A possible objection to this view might be that if "the husband of one wife" means marital fidelity, how can a widow be called "the wife of one man" (as in 1 Timothy 5:9)? But the singular phrase there probably re-echoes Paul's concern that the widow not be young enough to remarry, since there could be a serious temptation subsidized by church support, and those who are "widows indeed" would be those with a reputation for chaste behavior that their past behavior in marriage reflected.

[19]Perhaps the earliest reference to the question outside the New Testament appears in the work entitled *The Shepherd of Hermas.* In that work (book 2, chapter 4), the writer, sometime in the middle of the second century (though possibly much earlier), argues that there is no sin in a mate remarrying after the death of a spouse. Perhaps reflecting Paul's sentiments expressed in 1 Corinthians 7, the writer goes on to maintain that if one refrains from remarriage he can gain great "honor" and "glory." In so doing the early writer unfortunately moves away from the carefully stated words of the apostle and perhaps steps into that "stream

of asceticism" that would eventually overwhelm the patristic church and ultimately produce the doctrine that first stated that bishops should never remarry and ultimately concluded that they should never marry. This propensity in the church to accelerate the negative beyond the teaching of Scripture, this tendency to "go God one better" continues to haunt the body of Christ. It is no doubt the major culprit behind the emergence of the absolute denial of high church office to one who, at some time in his past, may have gone through the tragedy of divorce, however innocently.

[20]A final thought: given the sad state of the marriages of certain evangelical leaders which have recently become public in print and over the air waves, it is safe to say that the church is in far greater danger of being led by men who do not love their wives than it is of being led by men who may have, at one time in their past, suffered a divorce.